One God, Two Faiths

What Do Catholics And Jews Believe?

A Priest and Rabbi in Dialogue

by

Rabbi H. David Werb & Rev. Francis Cloherty

ONE GOD, TWO FAITHS

Copyright © 2018 by H. David Werb and Francis Cloherty

Cover Design: MZ Runyan
Interior Layout: Ezra Werb

First Edition
ISBN: 9781980925880

To Linda Werb,

Whose buoyant spirit always brought us joy
and who is sorely missed.

Table of Contents

Acknowledgments

We would like to thank the following people who assisted us in our quest to write a coherent, interesting and meaningful text: Rev. John Ronaghan; Rev. David Michael; Professor James Kenneally; Rabbi William Kaufman; Wilfred Sheehan.

Many thanks to Bob and Bea Gormley, as well as Paul and Carmen Arnone, for their insightful comments. We are grateful to Donna Faieta, Meg Venuti and Kay Schuetz for their continued assistance in copying and collating the manuscript.

We are very much indebted to Rev. Diane Kessler, Naomi Towvim and Celia Sirois, accomplished religious teachers in their own right, who spent many hours with us perusing our manuscript and offering constructive criticism to help improve it.

Sincere appreciation is extended to Rev. Michael McGarry for his helpful insights and suggestions, as well as to John Gould for his grammatical corrections.

Additionally, we offer our gratitude to Dr. Sherry Werb Leffert and Ezra Werb for reading our initial text and offering editorial comments. Thanks, also, to Ezra Werb for all of his help in facilitating the publication of this book.

Special thanks to Linda Werb, of blessed memory, for

providing us with delicious, nourishing sustenance each time we met in Brockton during the many months it took to complete our work.

Foreword

by

Rabbi William E. Kaufman, Ph.D

One God, Two Faiths by Rabbi H. David Werb and Father Francis Cloherty is a model of Jewish-Catholic dialogue at its best. What makes the book noteworthy is the mutual respect that Rabbi and Priest have for one another, their ability to explain their faith cogently, and their sincere quest to understand the faith of the other. The result is a very informative book.

The format of the book is interesting. They have selected ten topics to discuss: Revelation, God, One and Three?, Messiah, Religious Authority, Sin, Salvation, Life after Death, Angels, Interfaith Marriage, and Evil in God's World. After the Catholic and Jewish views on these topics are discussed, they ask each other questions to clarify their common ground and their differences. As an example of their discussion, let us review their views on Revelation.

Father Cloherty emphasizes relationships. He says that we need God in relationships of love in family, marriage, and honest healthy friendships. He states that while public revelation ended with God's word in Jesus, "God still reveals himself to us through communities and individuals in day-to-day life."

Rabbi Werb emphasizes the ethical import of Jewish teachings. With great clarity, he presents a Jewish view of revelation. He succinctly explains the philosophical issue of revelation in these words: "How does God, a non-physical being, communicate with human beings on the physical plane?" He discusses the various Jewish views of the revelation at Sinai. Some take the biblical words literally that God spoke to Moses. Other more liberal views hold that the Torah embodies human understanding of God's language but not the precise language. Werb stresses the ethical import of revelation. The source of revelation is God. "When we reach out to others in love, by caring for the sick, poor, and downtrodden, we are doing God's work and fulfilling the intent of his revelation."

In addition to stressing the ethical import of Jewish teachings, Rabbi Werb provides comfort in his approach to the problem of Evil. He writes: "God feels our pain and shares our suffering. This gives us some measure of comfort." Werb also states that the other belief that helps sustain us is the hope for an afterlife.

To summarize: Father Cloherty and Rabbi Werb have succeeded in providing a better understanding of each tradition, illuminating the beliefs that Jews and Catholics have in common and contrasting where they differ. This book will encourage dialogue at the grassroots level in churches, synagogues, and religious schools. I highly recommend this book. It enhances our understanding of Judaism and Catholicism.

Foreword

by

Professor James J. Kenneally, Ph.D

One God, Two Faiths could very well be entitled, "One God, Two Friends." It is a fascinating, well-written, candid account in which a priest and a rabbi explore the differences and commonalities in their faiths. Such a conversation could not have taken place without the teachings of the Second Vatican Council (1962-1965), especially the document *Nostra Aetate* (In Our Time), which enabled persons of good will to overcome the suspicion and mistrust resulting from two thousand years of Jewish-Catholic history.

As Father Cloherty and Rabbi Werb explore one another's faith they reveal their own personal experiences that resulted in this collaboration. The result is a book that can easily be adapted for those engaged in Catholic-Jewish dialogue (it even contains discussion questions for such meetings), for comparative religion courses, and serves, at the same time, as a refresher for the faith of any Catholic or Jew – thus making ideal reading for Lent or in preparation for Yom Kippur. This conversation should not only lead Catholics and Jews to respect and appreciate one another's faith but encourage them to become partners in striving to establish God's Kingdom on Earth. The book is highly recommended.

Introduction

We first met in 1993 at Stonehill College, a Catholic academic institution in North Easton, Massachusetts. Both of us were attending a meeting convened by Professor James Kenneally, director of the Joseph Martin Institute. We were there to explore the possibility of forming a Catholic-Jewish Dialogue Committee. The impetus for this gathering came from a Holocaust memorial program that was sponsored by the Institute under Professor Kenneally's initiative. This was in line with the Catholic Church's position of building bridges of understanding between Catholics and Jews in response to the groundbreaking document written in 1965, *Nostra Aetate* (In Our Time), promulgated at the Vatican II Church Council (1962-1965) convened by Pope John XXIII.

Through the years the Catholic-Jewish Dialogue Committee expanded to include more local priests and rabbis, as well as a number of lay people from area Catholic churches and synagogues. Over kosher lunch in the Martin Institute boardroom, we discussed a wide range of topics that were of interest to all of us on theological, spiritual and historical grounds. We all got to know each other well and developed a feeling of trust and mutual admiration. This enabled us to speak frankly and forthrightly on any topic that was put on the table. These discussions continue today.

Out of this matrix grew our own close personal and professional friendship, which has been nurtured through the various programs of study, worship, homilies and sermons that we have conducted together for members of our church and synagogue. Our efforts were aimed at promoting mutual understanding and respect for our religious differences. We have not only led classes and conducted discussions, but we have also spoken from the *bima* and the altar at each other's houses of worship during Sabbath Services and Sunday Mass.

Quite often we met over lunch to continue our dialogue and pick each other's brain about what our respective traditions say about a particular topic and how this affects us personally. We found that, although our views often differed, much united us. From this we have decided to collect our thoughts and put them in writing in order to share with others the teachings of our individual faiths on a variety of topics. These essays are not meant to be exhaustive analyses of each topic. Rather, they are more of a summary of the beliefs of each of our religions. In so doing, we hope to provide a better understanding of each tradition, illuminating the many beliefs that we have in common and contrasting where we differ. We have purposely avoided certain themes that are controversial and have been dealt with by others, so as not to detract from our fundamental vision of faith and theological dialogue. We are also profoundly aware of the painful wounds of separation that have affected the Christian-Jewish relationship for the past two thousand years. Our prayer is that this book will unite us in our common goal of encouraging dialogue at the grassroots level in churches, synagogues and religious schools, with the hope that people of faith everywhere will reach out to each other in friendship, love and understanding.

In putting forth our work we are indebted to Pope Francis who, in 2010, when he was known as Cardinal Jorge Mario Bergoglio, Archbishop of Buenos Aires, wrote the book *On Heaven and Earth* with his good friend and co-author, Rabbi Abraham Skorka. For years they were strong promoters of interreligious dialogue in Latin America and wrote down some of their conversations in their book. Although their subject matter differs from ours, they have paved the way for us.

Rabbi H. David Werb
Reverend Francis Cloherty
Brockton, Massachusetts, 2018

CHAPTER 1:

REVELATION

A Catholic View

When we speak of Revelation, we are talking about God's self-revelation to human persons. How does that happen? By way of example I will share a personal experience.

On July 4, 1982 at 3:30 p.m. I was standing with two friends on the north rim of the Grand Canyon. As we approached that rim, which is 7,000 feet above sea level, we walked through pine groves that still had piles of snow left over from a stormy winter.

Before I embarked on this trip I read all I could about the Grand Canyon. I saw the pictures. I read of its ancient origins, its depth and width. So I thought I was well informed. But then, as I stood at the edge of the canyon as the sun was beginning to make its descent behind us, I was immediately overcome by the immensity before me, the vast space contained by the canyon and its beauty. To the right, in the near distance, rainbows bridged the canyon caused by rain showers. I became awestruck, fearful, and I began to cry out of control.

In that experience, I had a sense of God's presence and God's beauty that are beyond any human capacity to manage or define. In God's presence, we are not in control. We often can't even begin to verbalize that which is going on within us or around us. On that day, in that place, God had revealed Himself to me, but I knew that there was still more that I was not seeing.

In Saint Paul's *Letter to the Romans,* we read, "Ever since the creation of the world God's eternal power and divine nature, invisible though they are, have been understood and seen through the things God made."[1] That God can be revealed to us through nature and life is one thing. However, it is another matter entirely whether we are able and willing to pay attention to life, and what is happening around us and within us, in order to find God speaking to us there.

Catholic Christians turn to the writings of the Second Vatican Council (1962-1965) and especially, the council's *Dogmatic Constitution on Divine Revelation* (1965) as the most recent, comprehensive and authoritative church treatment of this question. It is our faith that God has and continues to reveal Himself through nature. God, also, reveals Himself through the *Hebrew Scriptures* (what Christians refer to as the *Old Testament*). This is particularly true in the story of His relationship with the People of Israel and in the writings of the *Prophets*. As Christians, we believe that God's final and definitive word to humankind was spoken in the person of Jesus of Nazareth, who we believe was our human brother and our God. The *Hebrew Scriptures*, the *New Testament* and the ongoing oral and written tradition of the Church through the centuries carry God's Revelation to us.

In the book of *Exodus*[2] Israel prepares to leave Mt. Sinai. Moses is weighed down by the enormity of the task of leading God's people to the Promised Land. God makes Moses a key promise: "My presence will be with you...." For me, this underlines the way that God revealed himself to Israel – as a presence.

It is our experience that the power of the presence of another, especially when we are heavily burdened, can be critical. When I am present with another person at moments of great joy, pain, or just insightful conversation, at least upon reflection, I become aware of God's presence, and this has a powerful impact upon me, strengthening me in my efforts to really be with that person. God becomes my partner, or better, I become His partner in listening and caring. However, unless we pay some attention to that One who is present for us and with us, it will be to no avail.

For Christians, the opening lines of the *Letter to the Hebrews* define where we stand in the story of God's self-revelation to us: "Long ago God spoke to our ancestors in many and various ways by the Prophets, but in these last days He has spoken to us by a Son, whom He has appointed heir of all things, through whom He has also created the worlds. He is the reflection of God's glory and the exact imprint of God's very being and He sustains all things by his powerful word."[3]

Christians believe that God has revealed Himself to us in many words and deeds and through persons. He wants to give His very self to us. Just as God was and is present to the People of Israel, so too, God, in Jesus risen from the dead, is present in the Church and the world.

We meet this God in many ways when we serve the poor, the immigrant and the marginalized.[4] We meet this God when we come together with others, including those who do not share our faith, in order to create a new world based on the values of truth, love, justice and peace.[5] We meet this God in relationships of love in family, marriage, and honest, healthy friendships. When Christians are gathered as church, we find God speaking to us in song, the reading of Scripture, the preaching of the Gospel and the celebration of the Sacraments, especially, the Eucharist. Sacred art, e.g., stained glass windows, statues and the crucifix can also be mediums through which Revelation, God's word, can be "heard."

It is my sense and experience that while "public

revelation" ended with God's Word in Jesus, God still reveals Himself to us through communities and individuals in day-to-day life. The content of public revelation is central as we try to discern who God is and what is God's will. However, it would be well for us to always keep in mind that God's intent in revealing Himself to us is always about His wanting to get into a relationship with us and to draw us into a community of love with one another.[6]

1. Rom 1:20

2. Ex 3.3:12-23

3. Heb 1:1-2, cf also Constitution On Divine Revelation, par. #2

4. Matt 25:31-46

5. Is 2:2-4, Eph 6:12-17

6. Constitution On Divine Revelation, par. #9

REVELATION

A Jewish View

How does God, a non-physical being, communicate with human beings on the physical plane? Jews believe that it is through the interchanges that God had with the biblical patriarchs, Abraham, Isaac and Jacob, as well as with the prophets. The greatest revelation, however, was to Moses and the Israelites at Mt. Sinai.

The *Midrash*, the allegorical interpretation by our Rabbis of the *Hebrew Bible*, states: "Not only did all the prophets receive their prophecy from Sinai, but also, each of the sages that arose in every generation received his from Sinai."[1] Furthermore, the *Talmud* teaches us that every Jewish soul was at Sinai to receive the revelation, even those souls who were yet to be born.[2]

Jews differ as to exactly what happened at Sinai. The *Torah* proclaims that God spoke to Moses "face to face."[3] Some Jews take these words quite literally. They believe that the Ten Commandments, as well as the entire Torah, were given by God to Moses when he ascended the mountain. In this Orthodox view, God dictated and Moses transcribed His words faithfully and completely. Others believe that only the Ten Commandments were given at Sinai. The rest of the Torah was written on scrolls during the 40 years wandering in the wilderness.

Many non-Orthodox Jews believe that the communication was not literal but inspired by God through the minds of Moses and the prophets. They transmitted God's revelation in written form through various books that became sacred. Eventually, these were canonized into the Hebrew Bible. Some believe that before the revelation was committed to writing, it was transmitted orally for many centuries.

One modern theologian, Rabbi Abraham Joshua Heschel, opines that "as a report about revelation, the *Bible* itself is a midrash."⁴ What he means is that the Torah embodies a human understanding of God's revelation but not the precise language. God has revealed Torah, but the Torah itself is our ancestors' best interpretation of that revelation in their own words. Heschel adds, "The meaning of revelation is given to those who are mystery-minded, not to those who are literal-minded."⁵

No matter which approach is used to understand revelation, everyone agrees that the source of revelation is God. In the modern world we still rely on this revelation to guide us in our everyday lives. We renew our relationship with God on a daily basis through prayer and meditation, observing the commandments of the Torah and doing deeds of loving-kindness. When we reach out to others in love by caring for the sick, poor and downtrodden of our world, we are doing God's work and fulfilling the intent of His revelation. When we work together with people of other faiths for a just, righteous society and for the unity of humankind under God, we are experiencing His word. When we witness the beauty, awe and majesty of nature we are overwhelmed by God's creative power and feel His presence. All of these activities establish for us a personal relationship with God. We feel close to Him when we follow His will and see His magnificent handiwork.

For Jews, study of Torah is a further important means of being in God's presence. We are taught, "Two who sit together and discuss words of Torah, the Divine Presence rests among them."[6]

There is a well-known story in the Talmud that tells of a non-Jew who wanted to embrace the Jewish faith. This man insisted that he would accept Judaism only if a rabbi would teach him the entire Torah while standing on one foot. First, he went to Shammai who threw him out, thinking the man insolent. Then he went to Hillel who accepted the challenge and said to him:

> "What is hateful to you, do not do to your neighbor. That is the whole Torah, the rest is explanation. Go forth and study it."[7]

From this we learn that the basis of God's revelation is to teach us how to live properly and decently with our fellow human beings, fulfilling the Torah's commandment, "Love your neighbor as yourself."[8] In order to do so, we must study God's message to us through the words of the Torah. This establishes a personal relationship between us and God.

We see, therefore, that continuous revelation and mystical experience of God are possible on a personal basis even today, although we are far removed time-wise from the events described in the Bible.

1. Midrash Rabbah: Exodus 28:6

2. Babylonian Talmud: Shavuot 30a

3. Exodus 33:11

4. Abraham Joshua Heschel, God In Search Of Man, p.185

5. Ibid.

6. Ethics of The Fathers 3:2

7. Babylonian Talmud: Shabbat 31a

8. Leviticus 19:18

QUESTIONS

Rabbi Werb: According to Catholic teaching, can people of other faiths experience God in the ways He chooses to reveal Himself?

Father Cloherty: That one could infer the existence and presence of the invisible Creator from the created world was a familiar idea in first century Judaism and in the world in which the *New Testament* writers lived. This can be seen in the *Wisdom of Solomon* 13:1-10. In his *Letter to the Romans*, Saint Paul issues a condemnation against unbelievers (for Paul, at this point, Gentiles) for their lack of belief in the God of Israel, which for Paul was self-evident in creation.[1]

The *Dogmatic Constitution on Divine Revelation* of the Second Vatican Council affirms that God reveals Himself[2] in nature to all people. In the first chapter, the bishops state, "God who creates and conserves all things by his Word, provides men with constant evidence of Himself in created realities."[3] This makes it clear that all human beings can experience God.

In the *Declaration on the Relation of the Church to Non-Christian Religions* (*Nostra Aetate*) the bishops of the council tell us that, "Throughout history even to the present day, there is found among different peoples a certain awareness of a hidden power which lies behind the course of history and the events of human life. At times, there is present even a recognition of a Supreme Being, or still more of a Father. This awareness and recognition results in a way of life that is imbued with a deep religious sense."[4] The bishops, speaking of other religions, take the position that they "often reflect a ray of the truth which enlightens all men."[5] Thus, they make clear that the experience of God's self-disclosure is available not only to Jews, but also to Hindus, Buddhists, Muslims and others.

1. Romans 1:18-22

2. Both Jewish and Christian faith traditions have used masculine pronouns when referring to God: This in no way can indicate that God is male. We want to refer to God in a way that indicates a person capable of relationship. So, in English our choices in referring to God are as It, She or He. The traditions have chosen the masculine pronoun.

3. Divine Revelation I, par.3

4, 5. Declaration on Non-Christian Religions P2

Father Cloherty: Does it surprise you how much Jews and

Christians share on this topic of revelation?

Rabbi Werb: No, it does not surprise me at all since we are both rooted in the same *Hebrew Bible*. Our primary beliefs about revelation derive from our reading about the revelation of God to Moses on Mt. Sinai in the book of *Exodus*. We also share the narrative of God's revelation to Abraham, Isaac and Jacob in the book of *Genesis*. Revelation is continuous in both of our belief systems. How that revelation clothed itself in new garb later in history is where we differ from each other.

What we both agree on, however, is that dedicating ourselves to issues of social justice and working for the betterment of others is helping to fulfill the fundamental mandate of Divine Revelation. When we unite our efforts together to that end, we strengthen God's presence in the world. We both concur wholeheartedly that love of God and love of our fellow human being lies at the heart of God's teaching to us.

CHAPTER 2:

GOD, ONE AND THREE?

A Catholic View

In a hymnal commonly used in Catholic parishes in the United States, there is a haunting and lovely hymn with the title, "God Beyond All Names." The stanzas begin with the phrases, "God beyond all dreams, God beyond all names, God beyond all words and God beyond all times." The last stanza begins, "God of tender care." In this hymn we have a strong emphasis on our God as mystery. Yet, we are reminded that this God of ours, who is beyond us, is a God who shows us "tender care." Our God is beyond us and yet, God is immanent, with us.

In 1983, Pope John Paul II visited the Synagogue in Rome. This was the first such visit by a pope in office since St. Peter. The Pope began his remarks with the greeting, "My elder brothers (and sisters) in faith." Certainly, the Pope was not implying that the Jewish and Christian faiths were identical. But he was giving witness to the truth that Jews and Christians share a common faith in the God of Abraham and Sarah[1] and the God that Moses meets in the burning bush.[2]

In the first meeting that God has with Moses, Moses asks God to define Himself. Moses wants to know God's name. In the Scriptures, to know God's name is to exercise some control or ownership over God as when parents name a child. To name others is, in some sense, to define who they are in their innermost self.

In response, God gives Moses an answer, which is no answer at all. This answer has been translated variously: I am who I am; I will be what I will be; I will be gracious to whom I will be gracious. Finally God tells Moses, "You shall tell the Israelites, 'I AM sent me to you.'" God then describes Himself as the God of Abraham, the God of Isaac and the God of Jacob. What seems to be clear in this exchange between God and Moses is that our God is a God who is to be discovered in our relationship with Him.

God, then, is mystery, but God is also revealed in relationship. Finally, in the Book of *Exodus* 3:12, God tells Moses that as Moses goes to Pharaoh to gain the freedom of the Israelites, He, God, will be with him. This immanent presence of God with Moses and Israel is later symbolized in the Ark of the Covenant and the Jerusalem Temples.

For us God is one, but God is, at the same time, three, not in nature but in persons. By nature we mean the "what" of something; to use the term "person" implies a "what" that is relational, a "who." For Christians, God is found in relationship. In the Latin or Western Church, ancient writers describe the inner life of God with the Latin "Circumincessio." The image here is of three intimates in conversation, perhaps on a circular bench in a courtyard. In the Eastern Church, the word used is "Peri-chorisis." The use of this word implies a joyful circular dance of three persons.

The experience of God as Trinity was early in the Church, but how the Church would finally articulate this experience was only settled at a Church Council in Constantinople in 381. When we Christians use the word Trinity or speak of God, we understand that we are trying to put into concept and word a mystery that is beyond word, concept or experience in any final sense.

This calls to mind a story told about St. Augustine, the 4th century Bishop of Hippo, North Africa (354-430). One day Augustine was walking along the shore of the Mediterranean Sea. He was pondering the mystery of God, who is one, and yet three: one in nature, but in persons, three.

As he walked along he saw a little child with a pail. The child was running back and forth from the sea and pouring the water into a hole in the sand, apparently dug by the child. For some time Augustine watched, wondering what the child was doing since, of course, as soon as the child poured the water into the hole the water disappeared into the sand.

Eventually, Augustine approached the child and inquired as to what he was doing. The child responded: "I am pouring the whole Mediterranean Sea into this hole." Augustine told the child: "Why, that is impossible." The child then said: "It surely would be more possible for this hole to contain the Mediterranean Sea than it would be for you to embrace in your understanding the mystery of God, one and three."

There is one practice that I have adopted that has helped me to experience God as Trinity and verbalize that experience as a Christian. It is my observation that many Christians in their practice of the faith and prayer appear to be Unitarian and not Trinitarian. They may give notional assent to the one God being three persons, but that seems to be as far as it goes. Many seem to be focused on one person of the Trinity, the Son or the Father, to the exclusion of the Holy Spirit. As a practical remedy, I would propose that we Christians, in our prayer life, address and engage each of these persons. My thought is that just as in any one relationship, "the feel" and the experience is different from any other, so too, is there difference in engaging each of the three persons of the Trinity. This may not be true in every respect, but each human person we engage in relationship has some characteristic, some aspect, that is unique to that person. In my attempts at taking this insight seriously for over 25 years in prayer and reflection, I found that as a Christian I instinctively went first to the Son, Jesus, my brother who is also my God. I experience Jesus as the one "with me." I found going to the Father in prayer to be a longer process. In the end, the experience of God as Father is of one who is "for me" or "on my side." My relationship with God as Spirit is less clear to me at this time. I need more time to let that experience grow in my heart and mind in order to be able to articulate it. Yet, others have verbalized the experience of the Spirit as energizing.

So, I believe that we need to be "porous" or open as we face God. God is a God to be found in relationship. God is the God of Abraham, Isaac, Jacob, Moses and of Jesus of Nazareth, beyond us and yet, with us. Our God is beyond names and yet, a God of tender care.

1. Gen 12
2. Ex 3:12

GOD, ONE AND THREE?

A Jewish View

For Jews, God is one and cannot be divided into any parts. This is the doxology that we recite twice a day, "Hear O Israel, the Lord our God, the Lord is *one*." He is one in number, as well as nature, and is not divisible into parts or separate persons, even as part of the whole. The medieval Jewish philosophers wrestled with the concept of God's qualities mentioned in the Torah, e.g. merciful, loving, forgiving, angry, etc., and agreed that these were mere attributes, but did not define God's totality in any way. They were never conceived to be individual persons within the reality of God.

Maimonides (Rabbi Moses Ben Maimon) spoke of God's negative attributes as a way of coming to an understanding of Deity. Instead of saying that God is merciful, we understand this to mean that He is *not* vindictive. If we say God loves, we mean He is *not* hateful. If we try to assign qualities to God, then we are defining His essence, which is impossible.

In Biblical times, Jews were confronted with pagan beliefs in a multiplicity of deities. The Egyptians, Canaanites, Babylonians, Assyrians, Persians, Greeks and Romans all believed in many gods. Polytheism was the accepted belief system. It didn't matter whether the chief of the Gods was called Marduk, Zeus or Jupiter, for it was the same essential mythology. Triads of deities were also common such as Osiris, Isis and Horus in ancient Egypt.

Jews proclaimed a totally different idea in the time of Moses, confirming the belief of the Patriarchs, that God is one and indivisible without any other deities to accompany Him. It is with this one, indivisible God that we establish our personal, exclusive relationship as did our ancestors of old. We pray to Him alone and abide by His teachings. Although, by accepted convention we have historically referred to God in masculine terms with feminine pronouns creeping in these days, by no means is God conceived of as a corporeal deity. God is neither male nor female. God is spirit, without gender or physical attributes. God is not flesh and blood in any way and does not incarnate Himself in human form, according to Jewish belief.

Judaism, under the authority of Maimonides, considers Christians, as well as Muslims, to be monotheists, helping to spread the teachings of God throughout the world and hastening the coming of the Messiah.[1] However, Judaism does not accept the Christian concept of the Trinity, which runs counter to the basic Jewish belief in the oneness and indivisibility of God.

1. Maimonides, Mishneh Torah, Law of Kings 11:10-12

QUESTIONS

Rabbi Werb: Do Catholics accept other Christians' understanding of the Trinity?

Father Cloherty: The direct answer to this question is yes. Christian theologians in the 20th and 21st centuries have been working and writing more on God and Trinity than in recent centuries. They understand that the God of Christian faith who is Trinity must become the everyday experience of Christians and not an abstraction held in thought and words.

For example, Greek Orthodox theologian Metropolitan John Zizioulas[1] takes the position that the human person is essentially a relational being. We are built to be in relationship with others as is made clear in the second chapter of *Genesis*, "It is not good for the man to be alone."[2] Zizioulas then makes the distinction between an individual and a person. (Some of this now is Cloherty not Zizioulas). On the one hand, we are all individuals, but we can be so focused on defining ourselves that we place lines/barriers around ourselves to define who we are and who we are not. An individual who is a person, however, has to be "porous," capable of absorbing the other in some sense or another. The three persons of the Trinity are in fact persons and not closed individuals. Their union is a model for human community. Zizioulas proposes that we think of God as community.

Applying this philosophical construct to God gives us some appreciation of the never-ending struggle we make as Christians to understand who God is.

1. Zizioulas, "Human Capacity" 410-11, Ibid, "Contribution of Cappadocia" 35
2. Gen 2:18

Father Cloherty: The religious language used by faith traditions points to an experience of God by our ancestors in faith. How do Jews use their religious language and rituals to help arrive at a personal and communal experience of the God experienced by Abraham and Sarah, Moses and the prophets?

Rabbi Werb: Rabbi David Hartman, a philosopher of contemporary Judaism, says, "Biblical Jews met God in history. Momentous events, like the crossing of the Red Sea, were occasions for intense religious devotion. When God's power ceased to be apparent in history, as during the Talmudic period (200 BCE -500),[1] a new spiritual orientation began to emerge that felt Divine Presence and love for God in the act of fulfilling His normative message."[2]

Through ritual and prayer we Jews link ourselves to the past and try to experience the same relationship that our forebears had with God. During the Holiday of Passover, we reenact in ritual form both the suffering of slavery and the exhilaration of freedom. During the Seder we stress that it was God who liberated us from Egyptian bondage. It was not just our ancestors who experienced the liberation but, in a spiritual sense, all of us went through the process and continue to do so today. Each of us experienced the subsequent Revelation at Sinai, as if we were actually there at that awesome moment when human beings encountered God for the first time as a community of believers. Interestingly, it is the custom of Yemenite Jews to dress up in ancient travelers' clothing with packs on their backs and take a walk, to reenact the Exodus in a more realistic manner.

The rituals of our holidays throughout the Jewish year help us to experience our history. On the holiday of Shavuot (Pentecost), we stay up all night studying Torah in preparation for the anniversary of Giving of the Torah as if we were personally there at Mt. Sinai. In the fall, during the Holiday of Sukkot, we live in booths outside the home for seven days to experience the Israelites wandering in the wilderness after the Exodus. The purpose of all of this is to empower us to work for the freedom and liberation of all people by remembering what we have gone through in our history. Working for social justice and feeling compassion for human suffering are, therefore, very high on the Jewish agenda. These rituals are transformative, trying to make us better human beings and inspiring us to work for "Tikkun Olam," Repair of the World. Cardinal Sean O'Malley of Boston referred to this Jewish concept of "Tikkun Olam" at the Interfaith Service in response to the Boston Marathon bombing of April 15, 2013, calling on all people to dedicate themselves to Repair of the World.

Our daily prayers invoke the memory of our forefathers and also bind us to them. We call to mind their personal relationship with God, which we hope to emulate. We read the words of the Torah and Prophets as part of our services to remind us of the intimate relationship of God with the Jewish people, not only in ancient days, but constantly renewed each day in our own lives.

1. BCE (Before the Common Era); CE (Common Era). Jews do not use B.C. (Before Christ) or A.D. (Anno Domini - In the year of our Lord).

2. David Hartman, A Heart Of Many Rooms, Introduction xx, Jewish Lights Publishing, Woodstock, VT.

CHAPTER 3:

MESSIAH

A Catholic View

It is my experience that Catholic Christians rarely involve themselves with discussions of the Messiah. To be sure, Christians believe that Jesus of Nazareth was the long awaited Messiah of the Jewish people. He made it possible for Gentiles to share in the promise given to Abraham, Isaac and Jacob.[1] However, any discussion of Messiah is usually a matter of "past tense." The coming of Messiah occurred over 2000 years ago.

However, there is a Christian belief that this same Messiah will come again. In the Nicaea-Constantinople Creed which Catholics recite weekly, we find the sentence: "He (Messiah-Jesus) will come again in glory to judge the living and the dead and his kingdom will have no end." Christians also believe that the Messiah is present in our lives today and in the community of the church.

The concept of Messiah is prominent in the prayers and

hymns for the four-week season of Advent (Latin for coming), which precedes Christmas. The season draws our attention to the prophetic era, when the Jewish people waited and yearned for a Messiah. For Christians, this period begins with Abraham and ends with Jesus of Nazareth. However, this season also directs our attention to two other "comings" – in the future and in the present.

First, it is our belief that Messiah Jesus will come again. This Messiah will bring all things under God's rule here on earth in a Reign or Kingdom marked by truth, love, justice and peace. Advent also asks us to direct our attention to the present. In the Gospel of Luke,[2] Jesus tells his disciples that "the Kingdom of God is among you." The Greek original can be translated "within you." During Advent we also reflect on the Jesus-Messiah who wants to enter into our daily lives. We are encouraged during this season to give ourselves over to regular periods of quiet, less frenetic activity and prayer. We do this in order to be able to more easily welcome this Messiah who wants to be our companion and to enter more completely into our hearts and minds. When this happens we will find ourselves better equipped to offer ourselves to the world as true servants of the Reign or Kingdom of God. For us, then, Advent has a three-fold focus: the past, the future and the present comings of the Messiah.

Attached to our belief in Messiah is our belief in the Kingdom of God or the Reign of God. This Reign of God or

Kingdom of God is mentioned 39 times in the four Gospels. Most Christians recite daily the prayer Jesus left us, the Lord's Prayer. In this thoroughly Jewish prayer, we pray to God, "Thy Kingdom come, Thy will be done, on earth as it is in heaven."[3]

The teachings of the second Vatican Council made patently clear that the role of the Church is to be a servant to the Kingdom. It is to be a community dedicated to removing blocks and barriers to the advent of God's Kingdom on earth. In his last letter, *Peace on Earth* (1963), Pope John XXIII encourages Christians to work alongside all people of good will – those who do not share our faith as well as those with no faith.[4] Our work is to hasten the coming of God's Kingdom where God's values of truth, love, justice and peace will mark all human exchanges, individual and between nations.

From a concrete, practical point of view I believe that our belief in the coming of Christ (or Messiah) in the here and now is key to a serious faith in Christ. In the late 1980's I regularly spent Saturday mornings serving breakfast at a soup kitchen in Boston. Typically 40-50 men, most of whom didn't look to be in good shape, would start appearing at about 6:30 A.M. Even though security was thorough, for some time my fear of these men kept me behind a counter making coffee and washing dishes. This totally restricted me from any interaction with our guests.

One Saturday morning as I drove to the kitchen I determined that my behavior was nonsense. I would make myself get out from behind that counter and just act contrary to my irrational fear. So I decided that my first foray would be to go out and pick up empty cups and used plates. With determination, I walked through the guests down to the end of the room. The first cup in sight was on a table in front of a young man who was probably 25 years old. He looked up at me with eyes that radiated calm and peace. As I reached for that empty cup, perhaps sensing my uneasiness, he asked, "So how are you doing today?" I don't remember what happened after that, but following our exchange my fears disappeared.

Driving home, I realized that Christ (or Messiah) was in the middle of that exchange. This, of course, is exactly what Jesus taught us. We find Jesus-Messiah as we serve the hungry, the thirsty, the homeless and the immigrant.[5] For a person to consistently and deliberately avoid those in need or to never discover this Christ who is always present in our exchanges with those in need, for me, raises questions about the depth of a person's faith in any Messiah, past, future or present.

Finally, I find it a most welcome thought that both Jews and Christians have the God-given vocation to await the Messiah and that our faiths require us, with God as our companion, to prepare the way for the Reign of God on earth.

1. There are passages in Genesis and Isaiah that suggest Gentiles are to be included in the promise made to Abraham (Gen 12:2-3; Is 56 - Is 60:1-4)

2. Luke 17:21

3. The Our Father or Lord's Prayer was spoken by a Jew (Jesus) and there is nothing in that prayer contrary to Jewish belief.

4. Pacem in Terris, par.158

5. Mt 25:31-46

MESSIAH

A Jewish View

In the Torah, the Priest is called "Mashiach" (Messiah), which means anointed.[1] Aaron was anointed with oil as High Priest by Moses, his brother.[2] Later in the Hebrew Bible, the King was also referred to as Mashiach because he, too, was anointed. The Prophet Samuel anointed Saul as the first King of Israel.[3] Subsequently, at God's behest, Samuel anointed David as King[4] in place of Saul.

In the prophetic period, many of the rulers violated their positions of sacred trust, acting wickedly and introducing idolatrous practices. In reaction to this vile state of affairs, many prophets, especially Isaiah, spoke about a time in the near future when a new ruler, descended from King David, would arise, establishing a kingdom of righteousness and justice.[5] In this era, nature and society would be completely altered. Animals would cease their predatory ways[6] and human beings would live together in peace and harmony, believing in one God.[7] The Jewish people would be redeemed from all persecution and would return to Israel, rebuild Jerusalem[8] and make it the center of world government.[9] Jewish law would be followed and crime would be obliterated.[10]

The belief that a great cataclysmic war between the forces of Gog and Magog (Armageddon in Christian thought) would precede these events is based on a prophecy of *Ezekiel.*[11] This was conceived to be the great battle between good and evil heralding the last days.

These ideas became especially compelling after the Jews returned to Judea from the Babylonian Exile in 538 BCE. They longed for a return to the days of the Davidic Monarchy and read the prophetic passages with renewed enthusiasm. They believed that one day soon these prophecies would come about. In *Isaiah* 45:1, the Persian king, Cyrus, who allowed the Jews to return to Israel from exile and rebuild the Temple, is referred to as God's anointed.

In the Talmud, all passages in the *Prophets* predicting a future King from the House of David are considered to be references to the Messiah, as it states, "All the prophets only prophesied of the days of the Messiah."[12] Prior to this, in the Hebrew Bible itself, the word Mashiach is not attached to these passages. It is only from the Second Temple Period (516 BCE-70) onward that the word Mashiach became popular when alluding to these future days.

Beginning with the book of *Daniel* and continuing in the books of the *Apocrypha* and the apocalyptic literature, visions of the end days started to be circulated. During this time, Jews became divided in their understanding of the nature of the Messiah. Some still accepted the idea that a human, charismatic leader would arise and be crowned King over Israel and the world. Many others started to believe, however, that this was not going to happen in a natural, evolutionary manner. Only a supernatural, revolutionary Messiah, sent from Heaven and performing miracles, could roll back the evil created by the Romans. Professor Daniel Boyarin, at UC-Berkeley, in his book, *The Jewish Gospels: The Story of the Jewish Christ*, points out that *Daniel* chapter 7 and the first century apocalyptic work, the *Similitudes of Enoch,* both describe visions of the "Son of Man" as a heavenly redeemer sitting on a Divine throne, beside God, waiting to be sent down to earth to save mankind. These descriptions of the Messiah molded the belief system of many Jews at that time and paved the way for the later Christian belief that Jesus was the one who fulfilled the ancient prophesies. The word Christ derives from the Greek word, "Christos," meaning anointed one, hence, Messiah. Before Jesus there were other individuals who claimed messianic authority, according to the first century Jewish historian Josephus.

In addition to the Messiah that was to issue from the line

of King David, the Talmud speaks of the Messiah Ben Joseph[13] who will re-establish Temple worship and will be slain. He will pave the way for the Messiah Ben David.

By the Middle Ages, belief in the coming of the Messiah among Jews reached an almost dogmatic level. Maimonides said the following in his universally accepted Jewish Law Code, *Mishneh Torah*:

"The anointed King is destined to stand up and restore the Davidic Kingdom to its ancient roots. He will rebuild the Temple in Jerusalem and gather together the strayed ones of Israel. All laws will return in his days as they were before. Sacrificial offerings will be brought and the Sabbatical years and Jubilees will be kept, according to all the precepts that are mentioned in the Torah. Whoever does not believe in him, or whoever does not wait for his coming, not only does he defy the prophets, but also the Torah and our Rabbi Moses."[14] Maimonides adds this interesting caveat: "Do not imagine that the anointed king must perform miracles and signs and create new things in the world or resurrect the dead, etc."[14]

Although the prophetic predictions remained unfulfilled, Jews never abandoned the belief that they would come to pass one day. Throughout Jewish history there have been those who were thought to be the predicted Messiah. In Rabbinic times, Rabbi Akiva believed that the military leader, Bar Kochba, was the Messiah. Many of his Rabbinic colleagues scoffed at this, but he remained steadfast in his belief. When Bar Kochba was killed leading a rebellious attack against the Romans (135), and with the subsequent slaughter of Rabbi Akiva by the Romans, this belief ended. In later times, Shabtai Tzvi (1666) caused quite a stir with his messianic pretensions. He gathered a large following among Jews who believed that he was the long awaited Messiah. The bubble burst when he converted to Islam in prison after pressure was put upon him by the Turkish ruler. For centuries, however, many of his disconcerted followers awaited the second coming of Shabtai Tzvi as the Messiah, when he would throw off the garb of Islam and reveal his true identity. In medieval days, there were quite a few individuals like Shabtai Tzvi who harbored messianic fantasies. Jerry Rabow, in his book, *50 Jewish Messiahs,* tells the stories of many of these strange characters.

In modern times, the head of the Lubavitch Chasidic community, Rabbi Menachem Schneerson, after his death in 1994, was proclaimed by his followers to be the Mashiach. Many of his loyal devotees still cling to the belief in his imminent return.

Today, Jews disagree in their understanding of the concept of the Messiah. There are those, especially among the Orthodox, who still believe literally in his coming and await that day with eager anticipation. Non-Orthodox Jews generally think that, rather than one unique individual fulfilling this role, there will be a Messianic Age. At this time, humanity as a whole will finally come to realize that it is only through mutual cooperation, respect and love that we can bring about the long awaited era of peace for all mankind.

The idea that *we* are in control of when the Messiah comes is illustrated in this parable from the Talmud:

"Rabbi Joshua Ben Levi found the Messiah at the gates of Rome tending to the wounded and sick. The Rabbi asked him when will he finally come? He was quite surprised when he was told, 'Today.' Overjoyed and full of anticipation, the Rabbi waited all day. The next day he returned, disappointed and puzzled, and asked, 'You said the Messiah would come today but he didn't come! What happened?' The Messiah replied, 'Scripture says, 'Today', if only you will hearken to His voice.'"[15,16] The Messiah is destined to come only if we follow God's teachings.

Another saying in the Talmud predicates the coming of the Messiah upon pervasive ritual observance:

"Rabbi Yochanan said in the name of Rabbi Simeon bar Yochai: 'Were Israel to observe two Sabbaths scrupulously, they would be redeemed immediately.'"[17]

The strong belief in the coming of the Messiah is best summed up by the famous dictum of Maimonides in his *Thirteen Principles of Faith*, which has become an anthem of the Jewish people, chanted even during the darkest days of the Holocaust:

"I believe with perfect faith in the coming of the Messiah

and, though he tarries, I still believe that he will come."[18]

Although Jews do not share with Christians the Messianic identity of Jesus, we do share in the hope that the Messiah will eventually come and that the Biblical prophecies will ultimately be fulfilled.

1. Leviticus 4:3, 5, 16

2. Leviticus 8:12

3. 1 Samuel 10:1

4. 1 Samuel 16:13

5. Isaiah 11:1-10

6. Isaiah 11:6-11:9

7. Isaiah 2:3; 11:10; Micah 4:2-3; Zechariah 14:9

8. Isaiah 11:11-12; Jeremiah 23:8; 30:3; Hosea 3:4-5

9. Isaiah 2:2-4; 11:10; 42:1

10. Zephaniah 3:13

11. Ezekiel 38-39

12. Sanhedrin 9a.

13. Sukkah 52a

14. Laws Of Kings 11

15. Psalm 95:7

16. Sanhedrin 98a

17. Shabbat 118b

18. Commentary to the Mishneh, Tractate Sanhedrin, Chapter 10

QUESTIONS

Rabbi Werb: Why didn't Jesus establish the "future" Kingdom in his first coming?

Father Cloherty: In Catholic Christian faith, Jesus does establish the Kingdom of God or the Reign of God in principle. Perhaps better and more precise language would be to say that Jesus announced and inaugurated this Kingdom or Reign. Jesus proclaims that "the Reign of God has come near."[1] This is, of course, the present tense. So, as Christians, we believe that with the advent of Jesus, something in the human and world situation has changed radically and yet, we struggle with the existence of evil so evident in society.

As the expression of our faith has developed over the centuries, more and more we realize that the work of creation is not finished. We hold that Christian believers and all humankind are called to join God, to be co-creators with God of a universe and world society that matches God's idea or plan in creating.

Jesus presents to all the world a model or pattern as to how we work with God to create this new world. He does this through his life, death and by his resurrection. We also believe that baptism brings us into a community of believers that join the Risen Christ in the work of removing obstacles in ourselves, in the political, economic, educational and other systems in local, national and world societies that hinder the full realization of God's kingdom on earth as it is in heaven.

Despite the impact of Original Sin and the inclination to sin with which St. Paul struggled[2] and which we all experience, we still hold out hope for the Kingdom of God "here on earth as it is in heaven." We believe that God, working through and with the human family at a time unknown to us, will establish here on earth a reign of truth, love, justice and peace. The coming of Jesus, the Messiah, for the second time will signal and seal this event.

1. Mt 4:23-25
2. Letter to the Romans 7:15-20

Father Cloherty: How does the idea that Jews and Christians both share the call to promote the Kingdom appeal to you – that we are called to be partners in this work?

Rabbi Werb: I would be most delighted to see Jews and Christians working together to bring about a world of love, justice, harmony and peace. We both agree that this is the essence of God's Kingdom. It is not necessary for us to wait for the Messiah to do this. Every act of loving-kindness, every caring thought, every support that we give to others through charity, or just by lending a hand to those in need, helps to bring about

God's Kingdom. Judaism also teaches that we are partners with God in the creation of the world and we human beings are partners with each other in keeping that creation viable. Working together through social justice is one of the important ways that our beliefs unite us. When we strive together for Tikun Olam, Repair of the World, we help to bring about the time of the Messiah.

words and actions comprehensible to the world in which the Church lives. Our words and actions must be seen as those of a servant Church that lives at a specific point in history.

There are, however, certain people in the Church who are religious authorities. They teach authoritatively and determine, with the guidance of the Spirit, what is, in fact, the tradition of the Church and what is not. This function is especially important as societies and cultures change and as the faith develops in response to those changes from age to age (e.g. the role of the laity in the Church and the way we understand the presence of God).[3] And while there can be, and is, a wide range in practice and approaches to passing on the faith, there are still boundaries beyond which someone or some group has to say that this is not the tradition.

This role or function belongs to Church Councils, the pope and local bishops in their own dioceses. Local pastors, theologians, scripture scholars and religious educators, while they are authentic teachers, are only so in as much as they teach and preach within the tradition.

Since the Holy Spirit is the final guarantor and authority of orthodox teaching in the church, we can be certain that the faith given first to the apostles has reached us despite certain religious leaders. This is apparent in our reading of church history.

1. cf. Dogmatic Constitution on Divine Revelation #10

2. 1 Cor 15:3-5

3. Since the 2nd Vatican Council (1962-65) most would agree that the role of the laity in the Church has expanded and we now have clearer teaching that the presence of God and knowledge of God is not confined to the Church.

RELIGIOUS AUTHORITY
A Jewish View

The *Torah* is the center of all Jewish law. In Biblical times, the priests and the prophets were the primary authorities on how the Torah was to be observed. During the rabbinic period, 2,000 years ago, authority resided with the Sanhedrin. This was a body of rabbis, twenty-three in number, who served as judges in all matters of religious and secular law. The Sanhedrin also interpreted the laws of the Torah. The Great Sanhedrin, numbering seventy-one scholars, was convened to deal with matters of national concern such as a declaration of war and also served as a court of appeal. Lesser courts of three were established to decide matters of civil law. Additionally, there were many Schools of Study headed by prominent rabbis who interpreted the law and set precedent for the application of the teachings of the Torah. Sometimes these Schools came up with conflicting interpretations of Jewish law that were not resolved until later generations of rabbis decided which interpretation was to be followed. In a curious story found in the Talmud, where these legal discussions are recorded, the following is related:

"For three years there was a dispute between the School of Hillel and the School of Shammai on a particular matter of Jewish law, the former asserting, 'The law is in accordance with our views,' and the latter stating, 'The law is in agreement with our views.' Then a voice from heaven, announced, 'These and those are both the words of the living God,' adding, 'but the law is according to the ruling of the School of Hillel.'"[1]

The *Shulchan Aruch*, composed in the 16th century, embodies the historically evolved rulings of Jewish law at that time of both the Sephardic (Jews of the Iberian Peninsula) and Ashkenazic (Jews of European lineage) communities. Other law codes also came to prominence both before the *Shulchan Aruch* and after.

Contemporary rabbis base their interpretations of Jewish Law on the writings, legal opinions and precedents of the Talmud and the great rabbinic Law Codes that are based on the Bible and Talmud.

1. Babylonian Talmud, Eruvin 13B

QUESTIONS

Rabbi Werb: How much latitude does the local parish priest have in interpreting and applying Church law?

Father Cloherty: Perhaps the two most common ways that priests in a parish find themselves interpreting and applying Church law are through dispensations and in confessional matters.

Dispensation

On Ash Wednesday and every Friday during Lent, all Catholics are to abstain from eating meat as a penance for sin. This obligation begins at age seven.

One example of a dispensation would be when, for a good reason, a pastor dispenses his parishioners or a group of people gathering within his parish boundaries from church law. A good reason could be the following: a major tribute to a public official that is to be held and the food has been bought and prepared, but the organizers forgot about the abstinence rule for Lenten Fridays.

Some dispensations of Church law are reserved to the bishop. For example, a Catholic wishes to marry a Jew, Hindu or even a person with no faith. (Church law requires that Catholics marry Catholics.) In these cases, an exception (dispensation) can be made on a case-by-case basis at the discretion of the bishop. There are also certain sins that are only forgiven by the pope; for example, for a priest who reveals what he heard in confession, the Sacrament of Reconciliation.

Interpret

There may be a rule, but for a good reason the law does not apply to the person in a particular situation. For example, Catholics have a serious obligation to celebrate the Eucharist every Sunday. However, the obligation does not apply to a person suffering from pneumonia. Another example: for people to begin receiving the Eucharist, they must have an understanding of the Eucharist. Children with Down's Syndrome are welcome at the Eucharist even though they may have very little understanding of what they are receiving. A third example is that to receive the Sacrament of Reconciliation, formerly called Confession, the Church's celebration of God's forgiveness through the Church, Church law requires that a person tells his/her sins, orally or in written form. This is not required of stroke victims who cannot do either. No one is held to the impossible.

Father Cloherty: There seems to be no central authority within Judaism, either in the Orthodox, Conservative, Reform or Reconstructionist communities. This being the case, how does a

Jew decide what is legitimate religious faith and practice?

Rabbi Werb: After the Biblical period, legal authority was vested in the Sanhedrin and in the numerous schools of rabbinic teachers. Following the destruction of the Second Temple in the year 70, religious authority was derived from the rulings and teachings of the Talmudic rabbis. Down through the subsequent centuries Jewish practice was codified by the leading rabbis of each generation based on their interpretations of Talmudic law. The various rabbinic bodies of the modern branches of Judaism (Orthodox, Conservative, Reform and Reconstructionist) each has its own legislative commission to deal with contemporary applications of Jewish law that may have been unforeseen in ancient times.

Finally, it is up to the individual to either study the law for himself/herself or follow the teachings and decisions of his/her rabbi or rabbinic body.

CHAPTER 5:

SIN

A Catholic View

At the most basic level, sin is the harming or the destruction of a relationship. All sin, in one way or another, harms our relationship with God, others, self and even creation. This is the message found in the second and third chapters of *Genesis*.

The story of the Garden of Eden, which may be interpreted as an allegory, tells us that God created a relational world. In that garden, God, Eve, Adam and all creation lived in peace and intimacy. There was no need for barriers or protection. God placed Adam and Eve in charge of all that He created.[1] The one commandment that Adam and Eve were required to observe was that they were not to eat of the fruit of the tree of good and evil.[2] The man and woman were to live with limits. They were God's image but not God. They were to be accountable to that "Other," their Creator.

When they chose to ignore that limit in an attempt to be

their own God, two things happened. First, they experienced shame before each other and so they created barriers, in this case, garments, for themselves.[3] They were no longer comfortable being totally unprotected in front of each other. Second, they hid from God.[4] They no longer felt comfortable in God's presence. Their hiding themselves from God lets us know that the free, unprotected, intimate relationship they had with God and each other has been severely damaged.

It is our personal experience that when we have offended or deeply hurt someone, we begin to sense a need to protect ourselves from possible retaliation and the other person, depending on the degree of hurt, will stop leaving himself/herself unprotected when we are with that person. When we know that we have violated our relationship with God – by harming one whom God created in His own image, by a self-centered life style, by refusing to give God His proper place in our lives or by destroying a part of God's creation – our shame places a barrier between ourselves and God. It becomes difficult to be open and unprotected before God.

Further, to be in this state, where we effectively wall God and others out of our lives, negatively impacts and harms our image of ourselves. We wall out our truer, deeper self, created in God's image. When self, God and others are walled out of a person's life, that person is in a state of sin.

Catholics use the term "mortal" and "venial" to

distinguish the gravity of sin. Mortal sin destroys the ability to love in the heart of a person because of a grave violation of God's law. It turns a person away from God. One who commits a mortal sin prefers an inferior good to God. Venial sin allows the ability to love to remain alive in a person's heart even though it wounds it.[5]

In order to have committed a mortal sin, certain conditions must be met. This sin is one whose object is a grave matter, committed with full knowledge of its gravity and with deliberate consent.[6] If one has committed a mortal sin, reconciliation is required with the persons offended, God and the Church community. Normally, Catholics who have committed a mortal sin are required to approach the Sacrament of Reconciliation before receiving the Sacraments of the Church.

A venial sin harms a relationship but does not destroy it. An example would be a deeply committed married couple where one of the partners says or does something through lack of attention, which hurts the other. There is no requirement to confess venial sins in the Sacrament of Reconciliation. Much of what happens in the practice of the sacrament is spiritual direction or counseling.

For Catholic Christians, the way Jesus lived and died, the Ten Commandments, the Scriptures, and the teachings of the Church afford guidance that help us live lives that respect the holiness of our relationships with God, others, self, and all creation. As a person chooses to do or say something, the final guide must be conscience, but at the same time, each person has a responsibility to form her/his conscience properly, using good reason and the guidance of the teaching of the Church and Scripture.

The heart of teaching on Christian morality and right living can be found in Chapter 22:35-40 of Matthew's Gospel. Here Jesus makes it clear that all people are righteous before God if they love God, neighbor (which for Christians means everyone, enemy included) and self. We sin when we think and act only for ourselves regardless of how that affects others and our relationships with them.

In Christian moral thought, there is another sinfulness that we might label "cosmic" in that it hangs over all creation. While in the Catholic view, creation, including humanity, has not lost its fundamental goodness, human sinfulness mars all creation. We see references to this wider or cosmic sinfulness in Paul's *Letter to the Romans*, Chapter 8:19-23 and in the *Letter to the Ephesians*, Chapter 6:10-12.

Ultimately, we believe that only God forgives sin. Only God heals the destruction of relationships caused by our sinfulness. This is true whether the destruction is of an individual human relationship or the destruction of an individual's relationship with the wider community or with nature.

In the church, through the Sacrament of Reconciliation

or Confession, we celebrate God's forgiveness and healing of human sinfulness. The proper use of this sacrament by an individual presumes true sorrow, an intention to amend one's ways and a resolve to repair the damage done to relationships as much as possible. While Catholics are required to use the Sacrament of Reconciliation when they have committed mortal or grievous sin in order to participate in the life of the church, we fully understand that God's forgiving action cannot be confined to any church action or ritual.

1. Gen 1:15
2. Gen 2:16, 17
3. Gen 3:7
4. Gen 3:8
5. Catechism of the Catholic Church #1854, #1855
6. Catechism #1857

SIN

A Jewish View

In Judaism we believe that everyone is born clean and without sin. We recite daily in our morning prayers, "The soul that You have given me is pure." However, we do have the concept of sin. The Hebrew word for sin is "Chayt."[1] This originates from the metaphor of shooting an arrow and missing the mark. The farther from the center of the target that your arrow lands, the farther away you are from God who is at the center. In Judaism, a sin is essentially not living up to your religious potential and your own expectations. This distances you from God. Although there are punishments recorded in the Torah for disobeying the commandments, most of these are administered by God in his own good time.

Of course, there is always expiation, repentance and forgiveness for religious violations. The holiday of Yom Kippur, the Day of Atonement, serves to bring about such forgiveness for religious sins between us and God. Sins committed against others, which are also sins against God, can only be forgiven if we ask pardon from the wronged party first. We must also make restitution for any monetary loss we have caused. Thus, we must really go out of the way, expending personal energy, to repair a broken relationship with another person.

In our daily prayers, three times a day, we confess our sins asking God to forgive us. Our prayers for forgiveness are always couched in the plural because we pray on behalf of ourselves, as well as the entire Jewish community. This is also an acknowledgement that when we do something wrong it reflects negatively not only upon us, but also, on the community as a whole.

When Moses ascends Mount Sinai the second time, after the sin of the Golden Calf, God tells him that He is a God of mercy and compassion, forgiving sin.[2] Rabbenu Tam, a renowned twelfth century French Jewish scholar, based on a discussion in the Talmud[3] regarding this Biblical passage, delineated 13 attributes of God's mercy which center mainly on God's compassion and forgiveness of sin.

In Biblical times, atonement for sins was accomplished through the sacrificial system. There were various offerings prescribed for willful sins and accidental transgressions, as well as group and individual wrongdoing. After the Second Temple was destroyed in the year 70, prayer and good deeds took the place of sacrifices.

A story in the Talmud illustrates this notion quite well:

"It happened one day that Rabban Yochanan ben Zakkai was walking in Jerusalem with Rabbi Joshua. They arrived at the site where the Temple lay destroyed. 'Woe to us,' cried Rabbi Joshua, 'for this house where atonement was made for Israel's sins now lies in ruins!' Rabban Yochanan responded, 'We have another, equally important source of atonement, the practice of loving-kindness.'"[4]

In Judaism, each person is held accountable for his/her own wrongdoing, although others can innocently suffer from the evil that one person or group does.[5] This concept of individual accountability is stated clearly by the prophets. Jeremiah says, "Everyone shall die for his own iniquity; every man that eats sour grapes, his teeth shall be set on edge."[6] Ezekiel expands upon this:

"The soul that sinneth, it shall die; the son shall not bear the iniquity of the father with him, neither shall the father bear the iniquity of the son with him; the righteousness of the righteous shall be upon him, and the wickedness of the wicked shall be upon him."[7]

I would like to conclude this essay on sin with a story that my father was fond of telling and one which I witnessed personally as a child. One day, my mother, sister and I were out driving with my father at the wheel. All of a sudden we heard a siren and my father was stopped by a policeman for speeding. After my father produced his vehicle registration and driver's license, he explained to the police officer that he was a rabbi and a chaplain at the local penitentiary. We were all nervous about what would happen. The policeman, after looking him over and perusing his documents, eventually accepted his excuse for driving a bit over the speed limit and said to him in a stern voice:

"Rabbi, I am going to let you go this time but 'go and sin no more.'"

I like this story, not only because my father avoided a speeding ticket, but also because of the irony of the situation. In quoting a passage from the *New Testament*[8] to a rabbi, the police officer, in his exhortation, was raising Christian-Jewish relations to a new level. The lesson inherent in this story is that sin is something that we are all guilty of and absolving ourselves from sin is the task of all of us.

1. "ch" in Hebrew is pronounced gutturally as in challah, Chanukah or Bach.

2. Exodus 34:6-7

3. Babylonian Talmud, Rosh Hashanah 17B

4. Avot d'Rabbi Natan 4:21

5. Deuteronomy 24:16

6. Jeremiah 31:30

7. Ezekiel 18:20

8. John 8:11

QUESTIONS

Father Cloherty: How do Jews interpret the story of Adam and Eve in the Garden of Eden in terms of its fundamental message?

Rabbi Werb: The story of the Garden of Eden can be taken literally or allegorically. Either way, it tells us the same truths. God gives us commandments to fulfill. When we don't follow His desire, we suffer. In the Biblical story, the commandment is "do not eat from the fruit of the Tree of Knowledge."[1] When Adam and Eve disobey, they are punished by losing the potential for perfection that the Garden offers. They have to work very hard to achieve that which was previously readily available to them. They become separated from each other and from God. In the Garden, they are naked like innocent, immature children.

Once they have adult knowledge, resulting from eating of the fruit, they attain adult perceptions of each other and they cover their nakedness. The Tree of Knowledge of Good and Evil stands for all knowledge, including sexual awareness and mature wisdom. It signifies adult responsibility and action. Adam and Eve are every man and woman. They are all of us, and each of us, in our precarious existence. The story teaches us that in order to remain in God's presence and exercise our full potential as human beings, we must follow His commandments and obey His teachings.

Once the man and woman are evicted from the Garden, they are separated from God's protection and murder enters the scene. Brother kills brother. God says to Cain, "Sin crouches at the door and its desire is for you, but you can rule over it."[2] However, Cain sins, killing his brother, Abel, and is duly punished by God. Cain and Abel represent the filial relationship of one human being with another. When we close our minds to God and disobey Him, we end up sinning and wreaking havoc upon our fellow human beings. We are held responsible for our actions by God's law and human law, and we suffer the consequences when we stray. Our obligation as human beings is to recreate the harmonious conditions of the Garden of Eden by restoring our relationship with God and following His commandments. We must also maintain our relationships with others in a loving, ethical and moral manner. All people are part of the same human family, and we are interrelated going back to creation. Our striving for the Messianic age is essentially a desire to restore the spiritual conditions of the Garden of Eden and bring us back full circle to God's idyllic creation.

1. Gen. 2:17
2. Ibid., 4:7

Rabbi Werb: What is Original Sin and how do Catholics make amends for it?

Father Cloherty: "The account of the fall in *Genesis* 3 uses figurative language, but affirms a primeval event, a deed that took place at the beginning of the history of the human race."[1] For people of Christian faith, this means that, although the event and its form are lost to history, we believe that moral evil and human sinfulness is rooted in an initial human sin that has impacted all subsequent generations of the human family.[2]

Original Sin is not personal sin. One has a personal responsibility to make reparation for personal sin. We acknowledge it and then try to heal the hurt or injury to another caused by us. In an evolving understanding of Original Sin, there is a growing awareness that, as we look to the past, sometimes the policies, laws and actions of our ancestors, class or society or the nation itself have directly or indirectly harmed others and inadvertently encouraged the economic and social status in which we find ourselves today. In the name of national security and responding to irrational fear of the "yellow peril" across the United States, the U.S. government interned U.S. citizens of Japanese ancestry during the Second World War. Then, too, African-Americans provided free slave labor to raise food and to construct even our U.S. Capitol while they were denied civil rights and citizenship for almost 250 years. This was followed by still another 100 years of prejudice, inferior schools, segregation and denial of voting rights after emancipation. These historical events impact us today. Inequalities still continue to exist despite the fact that we have had an African-American president.

In an attempt to define a very complex reality simply, perhaps, we might call Original Sin originating sin. We would hold that there was an original sin by an individual or individuals of the past that triggered evil repercussions throughout human history, i.e. a distorted view of people who are different leading to institutionalized slavery, internment of Japanese citizens during World War II and the Nazi Holocaust. It is widely recognized today that the Holocaust or Shoah would probably not have occurred if it were not for 18 centuries of supercessionist[3] and anti-Semitic teaching in Christian societies. These teachings and unchallenged prejudices laid the groundwork for these atrocities and dulled our consciences.

However, as Catholic Christians we would hold to a further and more fundamental inclination to sin that is passed on to us all just by our being born as humans. St. Paul alludes to this tendency in his Letter to the Romans where he says: "I do not do what I want, but I do the very thing I hate... I see in my members another law at war with the law of my mind, making me captive to the law of sin that dwells in my members."[4]

The Council of Trent in the 16th century taught that Original Sin is passed on from generation to generation "by propagation and not imitation." So, this tendency to sin rooted in human nature is not just about influences from our environment, although environment can obviously encourage or diminish the power of this human inclination.[5]

The Sacrament of Baptism and the other Sacraments of initiation, Confirmation and Eucharist, bring one into the church community. This community supports us on the road to holiness as we strive to overcome in ourselves and society the impact of inordinate desire and Original sin.

1. Catechism of the Catholic Church #390

2. For more on this see "A Catholic View of Sin" above, Chapter 7 of this volume and Chapter 10

3. Supercessionism is the concept that Christians have superseded or taken the place of Jews in God's favor. Accordingly, Jews are no longer God's chosen people.

4. Romans 7:14-24

5. "World War Z" and the Council of Trent by Fr. Robert Barron, The Pilot 8/02/13 p.14

CHAPTER 6:

SALVATION

A Catholic View

The notion of salvation, as Christians understand it, is described as "to be taken out of a dangerous situation in which one risked perishing."[1] The Hebrew roots of the concept of salvation are spoken of in terms of our human experience of "protection, liberation, ransom, cure and health, life and peace."[2]

For Catholic Christians, salvation is fundamentally about our relationship with God. However, our salvation by God is also connected to our relationship with "the neighbor"[3] and increasingly, today, with all creation.[4]

In creation, God invited our first parents to "intimate communion with himself and clothed them with resplendent grace and justice."[5] This communion was destroyed by our first parents' sin. The fourth Eucharistic Prayer of the Roman Missal proclaims, "And when through disobedience, he (humankind) had lost your friendship, you did not abandon him to the domain of death. For, you came in mercy to the aid of all, so that those who seek might find you. Time and time again, you offered them covenants and through the prophets taught them to look forward to salvation."[6]

To be "saved" here on earth is usually a gradual process, whereby God draws each of us and all of us together to Himself and to one another with His love and peace. In its widest dimension, through the human family, this love is intended to touch all creation, animate and inanimate. This last aspect is concretized in our growing awareness, reverence and action on behalf of creation.

Christians see the whole Christ event (the life, death and resurrection of Jesus) as the ultimate event which demonstrates God's will and intention to save us all in Christ Jesus. In the 15th chapter of Luke's Gospel, Jesus plays out the unceasing effort of God to save all. He uses three parables: about a lost sheep, a lost coin and a lost son. In his outreach to the sinner, to the less than respectable and to the outcast, Jesus models God's persistent effort to save everyone despite all barriers and obstacles.

In the end, it is God who saves us. All we can do is open ourselves to God's saving action. God works through persons and events to promote and, if necessary, heal all the relationships we have as human persons. This work of God starts with us as individuals. God wants us to be at peace with our environment and deepest self, as we are, not as we would like to be. God desires us to be in mutual giving and receiving relationships with family, community and all of humankind. God wants us to be at peace with animate and inanimate creation, respecting and using the gifts of creation for the common good. Sin harms or destroys these relationships. Salvation, God's saving action, promotes and heals them.

Finally, the author of the *Book of Revelation* [7] presents the Risen Jesus (Messiah and God) as standing at the door of the human heart and knocking to gain entrance. One Christian artist depicts Christ standing before a door with no handle on the exterior. The implication is that the door of the human heart can only be opened to God from the interior. Sin is alienation from God, even potentially for all eternity. Salvation is freedom from sin, evil and all that blocks us from the fullness of life with God and one another.

" 'In His desire that all men should be saved and come to the knowledge of the truth, God spoke in former times to our forefathers through the prophets, on many occasions and in different ways.' Then in the fullness of time He sent his Son, the Word made man, anointed by the Holy Spirit, to bring good news to the poor, to heal the broken-hearted as the physician of body and spirit and the mediator between God and man. In the unity of the person of the Word, His human nature was the instrument of our salvation. Thus, in Christ there has come to be the perfect atonement that reconciles us with God, and we have been given the power to offer the fullness of Divine worship."[8]

A final note: Before the advent of the 2nd Vatican Council (1962-65), the sentence, "Outside the Church there is no salvation," was heard from time to time. Fr. Leonard Feeney, a former Jesuit, was teaching that doctrine widely and publically in the Boston area in the early 1950's. After several attempts to silence him, the then Archbishop of Boston (later Cardinal) Richard J. Cushing excommunicated him. Despite this action by Cushing, supported by the Vatican, there was no clear official teaching on the salvation of those who were not Roman Catholic Christians.

At the third session of the Vatican Council on November 21, 1964, the issue of how non-Catholic Christians are included in God's savings plan was addressed in *The Decree on Ecumenism*[9] and the *Decree on Eastern Churches*.[10] In brief, the bishops of the council came to see that there is one church entered into by Christian baptism although we are a divided church. We Christians are in communion with one another, albeit an imperfect communion.

On October 28, 1965, the Vatican Council voted to approve the document *Nostra Aetate* (*In Our Day*).[11] This was a declaration on the relationship of the Church to non-Christian religions. Paragraph four of that document addresses the relationship of the church to the Jewish people. Two sentences in this paragraph are key and foundational in current and future Jewish-Christian relations.

> "God holds the Jews most dear for the Sake of the
> Fathers: He does not repent of the gifts He makes or of
> the calls he issues - such is the witness of the apostle."[12]

From these two sentences flow a new dogmatic and pastoral approach of the Church to the Jewish people, i.e. the covenant that God made at Sinai with the Jewish people is ongoing and brings salvation; and more recently, the Catholic Church has no mission to covert Jews to Christianity.

In paragraphs two and three of this same document, the Church acknowledges that saving elements of God's truth and holiness can be found in all world's religions. Islam, Hinduism and Buddhism are mentioned explicitly.

From the above it is clear that the statement "Outside the Church there is no salvation" can in no way be held as the official teaching of the Catholic Church. Whatever popular beliefs or even teaching in the Church to the contrary has been rendered null and void by the authority of the almost 3000 bishops of the 2nd Vatican Council and Pope Paul VI.

1. Pg. 518, Dictionary of Biblical Theology (1973), Xavier Leon-Dufour
2. Pg. 519, Dictionary of Biblical Theology (1973), Xavier Leon-Dufour
3. Mark 12:28-34
4. Revelation 21:1-4

5. Dictionary of Biblical Theology #54

6. Roman Missal 3rd Edition

7. Revelation 3:20-23

8. Constitution on the Sacred Liturgy of the Second Vatican Council Parr. 3

9. Pg. 343 Council Daybook, Vatican II Session 3

10. Pg. 351 Council Daybook Vatican III Session 3

11. Pg. 191 Council Daybook Vatican II Session 4

12. Romans 11:28-29

SALVATION

A Jewish View

For Jews the concept of salvation is a very physical one. Throughout the Hebrew Bible, God promises the Jews that they will be "saved" from their enemies. These enemies are those nations that have conquered Israel or are threatening to do so. Peace for Israel and the entire world is part of this promise.

Salvation, in this sense, is national, as well as communal in scope, as is the outlook of most of the Bible. It is in rabbinic times, however, that the focus changes from the nation of Israel to the individual Jew. Even so, there is no hint in rabbinic literature of the concept of a personal savior. The Messiah is envisioned as saving the Jewish people, as a whole, from their oppressors. Each individual person, however, has the ability to save himself from sin by observing the commandments and coming close to God. An elaborate system of ritual observance developed to reach this goal.

"Hoshana," the Hebrew word for "save us," prominent in *Psalms* and in our prayers, has its etymological roots in a word that means make wide.[1] When we are in dire straits we are enclosed in a tight place. When God rescues us we are free to live expansively. God gives us victory. This is the underlying meaning of "Hoshana." Save us from the constricted place of physical threat and from the restricting effect of sin and wrongdoing.

Salvation goes hand in hand with redemption. The prototypical example of this is the liberation from Egyptian bondage as described in the biblical book of *Exodus*. We are taught in our tradition that we must always remember the "day of the exodus," the time of our redemption, throughout the generations. We mark this event daily in our prayers. In so doing, we are reminded that God is our great Redeemer and that enslaving and mistreating human beings is against His will.

In *Leviticus* 19:18 we are taught to love our neighbor as ourselves. One commentator explains that we should love our neighbor because he is like ourselves. No person is inherently better than another. All human beings, no matter their race or ethnicity, are equal before God and we must act accordingly by loving each other. God wants us to inhabit a world where peace reigns supreme. We can only do this by reaching out to our neighbors in love and maintaining a society infused with the ideals of justice, righteousness and harmony. The world is "saved" in this manner and the way for the Messiah is paved.

In recent years the idea of salvation has taken on a new meaning. Rabbi Mordecai Kaplan, the founder of the Reconstructionist movement in Judaism, speaks about God as "the power that makes for salvation."[2] In this regard, salvation refers to all the good qualities that we strive for in life that make us human. Our belief in God inspires us to incorporate these qualities into our lives and to bring about a world embodying these ideals.

1. Jewish Encyclopedia, 1906 Edition: Salvation

2. Questions Jews Ask: Reconstructionist Answers (New York: Reconstructionist Press, 1956), 83-84

QUESTIONS

Father Cloherty: Since the Jewish concept of salvation is so tied to the Jewish people and their covenant with God, how do Jews think about God's including all others in his plan of salvation?

Rabbi Werb: In our tradition we are taught that all righteous people have a share in the world to come.[1] The Jewish emphasis is on action and deeds, not just faith and belief. God's plan for ultimate salvation includes all people who do right and follow the ethical and moral way that He has set forth for us. We have the obligation to reach out to all people and teach them the values that bring about the salvation of the world.

We do not have to convert everyone to Judaism, however, in order to accomplish this. Righteous action is the emphasis, not right belief, although certainly, righteous belief leads to righteous action. For us, coercive proselytism is anathema because for centuries Jews have been subjected to forced conversion. That is why we don't have missionaries trying to spread the word. It is, rather, by our example of righteous and moral living that we hope to influence others to adopt God's plan for the world. This is not an easy task and sometimes we falter, but ultimately we hope to succeed in our charge to establish godliness among the people of the earth.

To spread the word of God's creative plan for the world is what we believe the Jewish People has been "chosen" for. In *Genesis*, we see that after each day of creation God says, "It is good!" He wants a world of goodness and we are His messengers to help bring this about. We seek to work hand in hand with all people of good will, irrespective of their religious faith, to establish salvation for humankind.

1. Tosefta Sanhedrin 13:2

Rabbi Werb: What happens in the afterlife to a person who is not saved?

Father Cloherty: In the Catholic tradition there are two possibilities: Purgatory, which is a temporary state, and Hell, which is final and permanent. In the past, Hell was conceived as a place with fire and physical pain. Today Catholics see Hell as a place of eternal separation from God "in whom alone man can possess the life and happiness for which he was created and for which he longs."[1] I conceive Hell as a place of total isolation and hopelessness, where no relationships exist. The church has declared that certain people are in Heaven. It has never said that anyone is in Hell.

However, I cannot resist including this story that was passed on to me:

"Everyone who ever existed is gathered outside the pearly gates as St. Peter prepares to read the names in the Book of Life. After the opening of the book he is surprised just how short his task is. He reads, 'Everyone will be admitted.' The ones who did not experience joy, but rather wondered why certain others were being let in, found themselves outside."[2]

1. The Catechism of the Catholic Church #1035

2. Story shared with me by Fr. Stephen Zukas

CHAPTER 7:

LIFE AFTER DEATH

A Catholic View

Belief in an afterlife existed in some form in ancient religions and in some Jewish writings before the birth of Jesus.[1] However, for Christians, the experiences of the Risen Jesus by early disciples, as passed down in the New Testament and Church tradition, are the basis for our belief in an afterlife. The early Church saw or heard from eyewitnesses and experienced the presence of Jesus Risen in various ways and places.

Christians observe Sunday in celebration of Jesus' Resurrection. On that day, most Christians celebrate the Eucharist or Mass. This is a celebration that places us at the events of Good Friday and Easter Sunday. This is very much in the spirit in which Jews celebrate Passover. At Passover, Jews, in prayer and ritual, join the Israelites who ate the first Passover meal ready to leave the slavery of Egypt for the Promised Land.

Christians do believe certain things about the afterlife,

but we do so with St. Paul's words very much in mind. Paul quotes an unknown author when he tells us; "What no eye has seen, nor ear heard, nor has the human heart conceived what God has prepared for those who love him."[2] That said, Jesus does use one image that can be helpful in connecting the afterlife to our everyday experience: the image of a meal, especially a wedding banquet, to which all are invited.[3] The ordinary experiences of family meals, meals with intimates, meals around family events and traditional meals where there is a larger gathering of family, e.g. Thanksgiving, Christmas and Easter, can give us hints of the afterlife.

In our Creed, we Christians refer to the Communion of Saints. We see this community or communion as embracing the holy ones on earth and the holy ones in heaven. For Catholic Christians, belief in this communion is part of our faith.[4] Our sense of connection with this Communion of Saints, here and hereafter, is at its highest point when we celebrate the Eucharistic meal.

Let me say something about Resurrection itself. That is what happens to us as we pass through physical death to new and eternal life. St. Paul tells us in his *First Letter to the Corinthians* that as we pass through death we receive a new body and a new spirit.[5] Paul parallels our resurrection with that of Christ. His argument to those who do not believe in our resurrection from the dead and our new life is that, if we believe in Christ's

Resurrection, then we must believe in our own, and if we do not believe in Christ's Resurrection, then our belief in our own resurrection has lost its foundation.

The Church canonizes or declares some of the dead to be saints and in heaven as models for our imitation. Franz Jägerstätter, an Austrian peasant, was beheaded in Berlin in August 1943 for resistance to the Nazis who then ruled Austria. He was recently declared a saint, yet many others who, as of now, have not been declared saints are considered to be so by many because their lives witnessed in some way to God or God's values. For example, Dorothy Day founded the Catholic Worker movement in the United States in the 1930's. Her concern and labors for the poor displayed God's preferential option for the poor. She has become a popular choice for sainthood in the United States. Many Catholics would also consider Rabbi Abraham Joshua Heschel and Mahatma Gandhi saints even though not declared so by the Church.

Catholic Christians also hold to a state of existence after life named Purgatory. We believe that Purgatory is a state and existence in which God gradually helps us to come to a total surrender to his overwhelming love for us. Another way to look at Purgatory is as a state of purification, where God helps us to let go of whatever is stopping us from being God's image, which is our original life vocation.

We believe that the prayers of the living can hasten the

total surrender to God's love that is required of those in Purgatory.[6]

Finally, Catholics believe in the possibility of Hell. This is a state in which eternal suffering for sin exists. That suffering in essence comes from a total lack of relationship. Hell is total isolation. The Church has never declared that anyone is actually in Hell.

Anthony DeMello was a Jesuit from India who died in 1987. He was well known for his writings and retreat lectures. He once told this story from a source unknown:

"To a disciple who was obsessed with the thought of life after death, the master said, 'Why waste a single moment thinking about the hereafter? But is it possible to do so? Yes! How? By being in the here and now. And where is heaven? In the here and now.'"[7]

1. 2 Maccabees 12:43-45

2. 1 Corinthians 2:9

3. Matthew 22:1-10

4. Catechism #963

5. 1 Corinthians 15

6. 2 Maccabees 12:43-45

7. *All Saints* - Robert Ellsberg p.242

LIFE AFTER DEATH
A Jewish View

Man's greatest fear is the fear of death. Judaism comes to soothe our fear with a belief in life after death. In the Torah we don't find any explicit teachings about the afterlife. Although Biblical Jews undoubtedly believed in it, they may have avoided writing about it in the Torah as a reaction against Egyptian belief in the elaborate physical afterlife of the Pharaohs. However, in the *Prophets*, the Witch of Endor raises the Prophet Samuel from the dead to speak with King Saul implying a belief in some sort of underground spiritual existence.[1]

Rabbi Neil Gilman, a contemporary theologian recently deceased, points out that under the influence of Greek philosophical speculation, most specifically the teachings of Plato, belief in the immortality of the soul started to take root in Judaism. He points out that the Apocryphal book, *The Wisdom Of Solomon*, and the writings of the ancient Jewish teacher, Philo of Alexandria, reflect an early Jewish belief in the immortality of the soul, based on Platonic thought.[2]

The first mention of an afterlife in the Talmud is found in the words of the great rabbinic teacher Hillel in *Ethics of the Fathers* 2:7: "One who has acquired knowledge of Torah has acquired for himself life in the world to come." As time went on, a belief in the immortality of the soul became deeply rooted. Two different realms in the afterlife, *Olam Haba*, were envisioned; *Gan Eden*, the Garden of Eden (Heaven) and *Gehinom*, the Valley of Hinom (Hell). There is a Judgment that decides to which place a particular soul goes. The concept of Judgment, along with Reward and Punishment, is related to the coming of the Messiah. However, it is not entirely certain whether the Day of Judgment precedes the Messiah, follows the Messianic coming or is reserved for the afterlife.

The eternal destination for the righteous souls after death is Gan Eden, the spiritual Garden of Eden. God created this as a physical place at the beginning of existence, and it was conceived conceptually to be the ideal spiritual place for the virtuous after death. It is generally described as a place of great joy and peace where the righteous sit at golden tables,[3] eat lavish meals together,[4] and celebrate the Sabbath.[5]

The concept of Gehinom comes from the Valley of Hinom outside of Jerusalem. This was a place in Biblical times where the pagans offered human sacrifices, including children, on fiery altars to their deities.[6] The idea of fire became the hallmark of Gehinom stemming from this abhorrent practice. Gehinom became the worst place that our ancestors could conceive of at that time. It became the metaphor for the suffering and punishment of wicked souls in the world of the spirit. According to traditional belief, the souls that are relegated to Gehinom only reside there a maximum of twelve months. After they are purged of their sins they go on to Gan Eden. The unrepentant wicked, however, are totally obliterated. Some hold that they remain in Gehinom forever.

Not everyone takes these descriptions literally. Rav, a great third century rabbi, proclaimed, "There will be neither eating nor drinking nor procreation, nor business transactions, nor envy, hatred nor rivalry in the spiritual world. Rather, everyone is pictured as sitting enthroned with crowns on their heads, contemplating the Shechinah, God's Indwelling Presence."[7]

Maimonides, in medieval times, expands upon this nonphysical notion of the afterlife:

"In the world to come, there is nothing corporeal, and no material substance. There are only souls of the righteous without bodies like the ministering angels. The righteous gain knowledge and the realization of truth concerning God, which they had not attained while they were in their lowly earthly bodies."[8]

The Rabbis tell various stories about the reality of the afterlife. One such story revolves around Rabbi Joseph who suddenly became ill and his soul departed. After some time, he returned to life. His father, Rabbi Joshua Ben Levi, asked him what he saw. He replied, "I saw an upside down world. People who were considered important in this world are below in that world, and people considered lowly in this world were elevated in that world."[9]

Over a period of many centuries, the concept of the soul developed further. In Kabbalah, Jewish mysticism, the soul is depicted as having five levels: *Nefesh* (Life force), *Ruach* (Spirit), *Neshamah* (Soul), *Chayah* (Living) and *Yechida* (Singularity). The *Zohar*, a mystical commentary on the Bible, teaches that when we die we are greeted by the souls of our departed loved ones and reunited with them.[10] In our day this has become an almost universally accepted belief among religious people of all faiths.

Orthodox Jews today still accept the traditional teachings about life after death. Other Jews are not united in their conceptions of what happens after we die. Many think that the soul goes to a spiritual place where the wrongs of this world are righted by God and that the souls of the deceased exist in eternal life. All of this takes place in another dimension of God's vast Eternity. Others believe that when we die, that is the end of all existence.

A corollary to the belief in Life after Death is the concept of resurrection. Resurrection is alluded to in the books of *Isaiah* and *Daniel*.[11] The Prophet Ezekiel describes extensively the future resurrection of the Jewish people after the destruction of the First Temple.[12] In commenting on this mystical vision in the Talmud, Rabbi Eliezer, the son of Rabbi Yose the Galilean, made an astounding statement: "The dead whom Ezekiel revived went up to Palestine, married wives and produced daughters. Rabbi Judah son of Bathyra said: 'I am one of their descendants and these are the tefillin (phylacteries) which my grandfather bequeathed to me from them.'"[13]

We find two actual incidents of resurrection in the Hebrew Bible, one with Elijah the Prophet and the other with Elisha, his successor.[14] In each case the prophet brings back to life a dead child. We also find individual cases of resurrection recounted in the Talmud.[15]

Traditionally, the resurrection of the dead was to take place in the Messianic age. Here, too, it is not clear whether resurrection precedes the Messiah or follows. Jews recite in our prayers, three times a day, the hope for physical resurrection. Reform and Reconstructionist Jews have altered the wording of these prayers because they do not believe in this concept.

Although modern science does not deal with the possibility of resurrection, one notable exception is found in the writings of Frank Tipler, a mathematical physicist at Tulane University. Tipler's speculation centers around the Omega Point, a singularity that he believes will exist at the end of time that will embody all human intelligence and will serve as a means for the resurrection of the dead.[16] Although many scientists are skeptical of his theory, it is interesting to note that resurrection is actually being discussed in scientific circles.

The idea of reincarnation, although not accepted in normative Judaism, is an important belief in Jewish mysticism as taught by Kabbalah. This teaching has become more popular today as Kabbalah has gone into the mainstream and is studied even by non-Jews.

Judaism is very inclusive in its understanding of the future world. We are taught in the Talmud, "The righteous of all nations have a share in the world to come."[17] Maimonides echoes this teaching in his law code, *Mishneh Torah.*[18]

In my early years in the rabbinate, I had occasion to visit an elderly congregant in the hospital. I had some trepidation about going into her room to talk with her since she had been diagnosed with terminal cancer and had only a short time to live. I thought I would find a person in a lot of pain, very depressed and rolled up in bed. What would I say to her? What words of wisdom could I offer her to ease her emotional burden? When I mustered up the courage to enter her room, much to my surprise, she was sitting upright in a chair, had a pleasant air about herself, and greeted me with a warm smile. As we got to talking, I quickly realized that her impending death was not distressing to her because she had come to terms with it. She was ready to die because she felt that she had lived a good, fulfilled life in this world. She was also prepared emotionally to accept her fate since she believed in life after death. I was very much comforted by her demeanor and attitude and realized the profound effect a belief in the afterlife has on our human psyche, helping us to counter our fear of death with a belief in life everlasting.

It is our fervent hope and prayer, based on traditional teachings, that the physical world that we are all a part of is not the totality of existence, but that God has prepared for us a realm of eternal life where we will be united with Him and with our loved ones who have gone before.

1. 1 Samuel 28:11-14

2. The Death Of Death, Neil Gilman, Jewish Lights Publishing, Woodstock, VT, Pp 105-112

3. Babylonian Talmud, Tractate Taanit 25a

4. Ibid, Tractate Baba Batra 75a

5. Ibid., Tractate Berachot 57b

6. II Kings 23:10 Jeremiah 7:31

7. Ibid, Tractate Berachot 17a

8. Mishneh Torah, Repentance 8

9. Babylonian Talmud, Tractate Pesachim 50a

10. Zohar, Vayechi, 217a

11. Isaiah 25-27; Daniel 10-12

12. Ezekiel 37:1-37:14

13. Babylonian Talmud, Sanhedrin 92b, Tefillin (phylacteries) are little boxes, with leather straps attached, containing passages from the prayer book, worn on arm and head during weekday prayer.

14. 1 Kings 17:17-24; 2 Kings 4:32-37

15. Babylonian Talmud, Avoda Zara 10b; Megillah 7b; Baba Kama 117a-b

16. Frank J. Tipler (1994). The Physics of Immortality: Modern Cosmology,

God and the Resurrection of the Dead. New York: Doubleday.

17. Ibid., Tractate Sanhedrin 105a

18. Mishneh Torah, Repentance 3:5

QUESTIONS

Father Cloherty: Is there a hierarchy of people in heaven? That is, are some people of certain faiths number one?

Rabbi Werb: Judaism teaches that all righteous people have a share in the world to come. This includes people of any faith or no faith. It doesn't matter what one's theological belief or religion is. What matters to God is how we act. Righteous, just and compassionate actions are the paths to heaven.

Rabbi Werb: Do Catholics believe that the souls of people of other faiths, who do not believe in Jesus, exist in eternity with God?

Father Cloherty: In the 2nd Eucharistic Prayer we pray to God for "all who have fallen asleep in the hope of the resurrection and all who have died in your mercy; welcome them into the light of your face."[1] In the 4th Eucharistic Prayer we pray to God for "all the dead whose faith you alone have known."[2]

Certainly today, Catholics believe that salvation or heaven is open to all. Without denying that Jesus the Christ is the

Way, the Truth, and the Life,[3] we believe that God's Holy Spirit and God's love are available to all people, even those with no faith. How that happens apart from faith in Christ is explained by theologians in various ways.[4] However, it is clear that Catholic Christians hold what the 2nd Vatican Council taught, namely: "His (God's) providence, evident goodness and saving design extend to all men against the day when the elect are gathered together in the holy city... and in whose splendor all people will walk."[5]

1, 2. The Roman Missal 3rd Edition

3. John 14:6

4. Redemptoris Missio par 10

5. Nostra Aetate p.1; see also Acts 14:17, Romans 2:6-7, 1 Timothy 2:4 and Revelation 21:23ff

CHAPTER 8:

ANGELS

A Catholic View

The word angel is not a name that indicates a nature but a function. The Hebrew "maĺach" and the Greek "angelos" mean messenger. Angels are "spirits destined to serve, sent on missions for the good of those who should inherit salvation."[1] In the Scriptures, angels are mysterious beings, non corporeal. Apparently, they can become visible to humans and speak in order to bring messages from God.

My thoughts on angels as a Catholic have largely been influenced by five passages in Scripture: *Genesis* 18 and 19, *Genesis* 32:22-32, *Luke* 1:26-38, and *Revelation* 12.

Genesis 18 and 19

In these chapters, Abraham and Sarah have an encounter with three travelers. In verse 2, they are "three men." In verses 17-32, the Lord, i.e. God, begins to have a conversation with

Abraham. Later, in verse 33, we are told that "the Lord went his way." Finally, in the first verse of Chapter 19 we are told that "the two angels" came to Sodom in the evening.

It seems that we could read this text to mean that what at first seemed to be three men turn out to be the Lord and two angels.

Genesis 32: 22-32

This story, like the previous one, is fraught with mystery and ambiguity. Jacob wrestles with a mysterious being, a man, all night, "until daybreak."[2] Later, in verse 30, Jacob called the place Peniel saying, "for I have seen God face to face."

I would note a similarity of contexts in these two texts. Abraham, Sarah and Jacob were all facing crises. They were wrestling with important, concrete life issues.

Abraham had no children by his wife Sarah. Abraham did have a child, Ishmael, by Hagar, Sarah's maid. However, for this son to stand as Abraham's heir was potentially quite problematic. It had to be a source of unease to Sarah and Abraham in their relationship with each other and as they looked to the future. The entrance of the travelers, God/angels on to this scene brings a happy resolution with Sarah's pregnancy and later, the birth of Isaac.

Jacob was wrestling with fear and anxiety as he prepared to meet his brother and twin, Esau. This was to be their first encounter since Jacob stole Esau's birthright and place in the family. By this time, Esau was a powerful lord and could choose to destroy Jacob.

Both of these texts assure us that when we face crises or pivotal moments in our lives, personal, family, and political, and when we wrestle with uncertainty and ambiguity about the future, God does not leave us alone. God is in the wrestling, and God sends angels in one form or another to challenge, assure and guide us to a resolution that will bring peace and happiness to us and to all touched in any way by the crisis at hand.

Luke 1: 26-38

"The angel Gabriel was sent by God... to a virgin... The virgin's name was Mary."[3]

We are not told how or in what form Gabriel appeared. We are only told that he was sent by God to Mary with an invitation, not an order or command.

God invites Mary to be the mother of the Messiah and Son of God. Mary is perplexed. She has questions. But what is important to notice is that Mary is free to say yes or no to God. When God invites us to be or do something, God always respects our freedom. As we see, Mary says yes to Gabriel. In doing so, she says yes to God.

Angels are mentioned in many places in the New Testament. In the *Gospel of Matthew* 18:10, the little ones, i.e.

children and those with no power, have angels. In the *Letter to the Hebrews* 12:2, unexpected guests can be angels in disguise.

Revelation 12

In Jewish and Christian traditions there is another angel, a fallen angel. In the book of *Revelation* 12, there is a war in heaven and the Archangel Michael and his angels fight the great dragon also called the Devil or Satan. That dragon, Devil or Satan is thrown out of heaven and thereafter, the war continues on earth. This Satan character appears as the serpent in the Garden of Eden.[4] He tries to draw Jesus away from his vocation to be Messiah.[5] Later, we are told that Satan was losing the battle as Jesus' disciples move out in ministry.[6]

If we take all of these scripture passages together, I believe we can get an impression that will take us back to the root meaning of the word angel – a messenger. Sometimes the angel is visible, sometimes not. Sometimes he seems to be a real human person used by God. However, whatever the form, the angel or angels are sent by God to help move us further along the road to salvation and doing good.

A good friend of mine spoke of being very seriously ill and losing his will to live. A young student doctor came by his hospital room daily and spent time with him. He would end every visit with the words, "I will take care of you." This doctor was not his personal physician, and as my friend's sense of hopefulness began to dramatically improve, he never saw that young doctor again.[7] Was that doctor an angel in disguise?

In contrast, the Devil, a fallen angel, can assume all of the forms of good angels as he/she/it entices us to follow the road that leads us away from God.

In some circles, there is a belief that at birth each of us is assigned a guardian angel to guide and protect us.[8]

Angels also appear at regular intervals in our liturgy and worship. At the beginning of the church year, the angel Gabriel announces to Mary that she is being called to be the mother of the Messiah. At the end of the church year, Angels appear with the Son of Man when He comes in judgment. At every Eucharist, before the consecration of the bread and wine, we are reminded that we are joining the angels and archangels, cherubim and seraphim in praising God.

1. Pg. 14 Dictionary of Biblical Theology – Xavier León-Dufour

2. Genesis 32:24

3. Lk 1:26

4. Gen 3

5. Lk 4:1-16.

6. Ibid 4:1-12

7. As told to me by Fr. Ronald Gariboldi

8. Matthew 18:10

ANGELS

A Jewish View

Cherubim guard the entrance to the Garden of Eden after Adam and Eve are banished.[1] Angels, however, are usually called malachim, messengers. Three such messengers visit Abraham at his desert home to proclaim the future birth of Isaac.[2] Two go on to warn Lot, Abraham's nephew, of the impending destruction of the cities of Sodom and Gomorra.[3] An angel calls out to Hagar in her anguish when she flees from the wrath of Sarah[4] and another angel stops Abraham on Mt. Moriah from slaughtering his son, Isaac, as a sacrifice.[5] When Jacob escapes from his brother, Esau, he dreams of angels ascending and descending a great cosmic ladder stretched from earth to heaven.[6] When he leaves his father-in-law, Laban, with his wives and children he encounters a camp of angels.[7] Prior to his encounter with Esau, many years later, Jacob wrestles with some sort of angel.[8]

The Torah is not clear about who these angelic beings are. They are usually depicted in human form. In the story of Abraham's encounter with the three angels, there is an element of identification with Divinity, because the narrative intersperses God's words with those of the angels. It is only in the later Biblical books of the *Prophets* and the *Writings* that angels become more clarified and take on a more prominent role. The poetic portions of the books of *Psalms* often refer to angels as doing God's bidding. They are depicted by Isaiah the Prophet as God's heavenly retinue singing his praises.[9] It is not until *Ezekiel* Chapter 10 that we see cherubim and other angels envisioned as being winged creatures. In the Book of *Job*, Satan is a mysterious character and is referred to as "the Satan," in the impersonal form.[10] In *Zecheriah* 3:1 the prophet characterizes "the Satan" as the accuser. It is only in the book of *Daniel* that two angels are identified by personal name, Gabriel and Michael.[11]

In Talmudic literature angelology becomes far more developed with names and tasks assigned to various angels and different categories of angels delineated. We are told that there are four angels that surround God's throne: Michael, Gabriel, Uriel and Raphael.[12] Two passages describe a cherub as having the face of a young child.[13] Even so, the belief in angels as independent, spiritual beings is not fully organized in Jewish belief. In Kabbalistic literature angels take on more importance representing extensions of Divine qualities.

Throughout the Middle Ages, belief in angels and demons took hold in the popular psyche and a whole range of spirits was imagined. This may have evolved from a world where Jews were strongly persecuted and led very cloistered physical lives in ghettos. They, thus, imagined a spiritual world beyond theirs that was more expansive, affording their minds a means of escape from the drabness, troubles and difficulties of their own existence. Even the great rationalist Maimonides counts 10 categories of angels.[14]

In modern times most religious Jews still believe in the existence of angels. References to them are included very prominently in the prayer book in our daily services. However, some Jews do not believe literally in angels because this would compromise the oneness and omnipotence of God. In this view, angels are metaphors and poetic intermediaries that bring us into the realm of Divine spirituality. They serve to bridge the gap in our minds between physical humans and a non-physical God.

There is a traditional belief that when we do a good deed, we create a good angel and when we do an evil act, we create a bad angel. These angels act on our behalf to lead us down the right or wrong path. They are essentially extensions of our own personalities. We become the angel. In this regard I would commend the reader to Dr. Ron Wolfson's book, *God's to-do List; 103 Ways to be an Angel on God's Earth*.[15]

In Talmudic legend, we read: "Rabbi Yosi ben Yehuda taught: Two ministering angels, one good and one bad, escort a person home from the synagogue on Shabbat eve. When he comes home and finds the candles lit, the table set, and the bed made, the good angel says, 'May it be God's will that it also be so next Shabbat,' and the bad angel is compelled to say 'amen.' But if the house is not prepared for Shabbat, then the bad angel says,

'May it be God's will that it also be so next Shabbat,' and the good angel has to say 'amen.'"[16]

On Friday night the universally recited Sabbath hymn, Shalom Aleichem, reflects this thought:

"Peace upon you, ministering angels, messengers of the Most High, of the Supreme King of Kings, the Holy One, blessed be He.

Come in peace, angels of peace, messengers of the Most High, of the Supreme King of Kings, the Holy One, blessed be He.

Bless me with peace, angels of peace, messengers of the Most High, of the Supreme King of Kings, the Holy One, blessed be He.

May your departure be in peace, angels of peace, messengers of the Most High, of the Supreme King of Kings, the Holy One, blessed be He."

Contemporary popular belief in angels is based upon these traditional teachings.

1. Genesis 3:24
2. Ibid., 18:1-15
3. Ibid., 19:1-14
4. Ibid., 21:17
5. Ibid., 22:11-12
6. Genesis 28:10-12
7. Ibid., 32:1-2

8. Ibid., 32:22-31

9. Isaiah 6:2-3

10. Job 1:6

11. Daniel 8:16; 10:13

12. Numbers Rabbah 2:10

13. Sukkah 5b; Haggigah 13b

14. Yad Hachazakah: Yesodei Hatorah

15. Jewish Lights Publishing

16. Babylonian Talmud, Shabbat 119b

QUESTIONS

Father Cloherty: My understanding is that current day Rabbinic Judaism finds its roots in the first century Pharisee party. Some current Catholic Scripture scholars believe that on some matters the message of Jesus hews close to the Pharisees' positions; for example, the belief in angels and the resurrection. What do you think of this?

Rabbi Werb: Rabbinic Judaism in Talmudic times, which developed from the teachings of the Pharisees, agrees with Christian teachings, in large part, on the meaning of angels. However, in our belief system there is no cosmic war between the angels. For Jews, Satan plays a very minor role except in folk myth. He has no independent power to subvert God and is not the polar opposite, as some portray him. For the rabbis, Satan was the symbolic embodiment of the evil spirit that exists within us alongside the good spirit. Every day, we are pulled in one direction or the other and it is up to us, through our faith and trust in God, to channel the good spirit that is within us. Satan has no real existence except in our own minds.

More than likely, Jesus was in line with Pharisaic belief in most of the teachings spoken in his name in the *Gospels*, even though the Pharisees are portrayed very poorly in the *New Testament*. For those interested in this topic, I would refer you to the book, *Jesus the Pharisee* by Hyam Maccoby. *The Jewish Annotated New Testament* edited by Amy-Jill Levine and Marc Zvi Brettler would also be helpful to read in this regard. The Pharisees were great rabbis, teachers and individuals who were part of a religious, political and social movement, one of many that existed during the later Second Temple period beginning around 140 BCE and lasting until the destruction of the Temple by the Romans in the year 70. The great rabbis of the rabbinic period that followed for the next four hundred years inherited their mantle of leadership.

Resurrection was definitely a belief adhered to in pharisaic and rabbinic times.

Rabbi Werb: Do Catholics pray to angels for intercession?

Father Cloherty: Yes. Catholics ask angels, as well as the saints and those who pilgrimage with us in this life, for intercessory prayer to God. Michael, the Archangel, is seen as one to invoke in the face of serious moral evil and temptation.[1] Raphael, whose name means 'God has healed,' is prominent as God's healing agent in the book of *Tobit* which is considered inspired and part of our Bible,[2] and in the Gospel of John.[3]

1. Revelation 12:7-9
2. Tobit 7:1 – 8:18; 11:7-14
3. John 5:1-4

CHAPTER 9:

INTERFAITH MARRIAGE

A Catholic View

For Catholic Christians, and some other Christians, marriage is a sacrament whereby a baptized woman and a baptized man enter into a new relationship with each other and with the Church community. They become a sign of Christ to each other and a sign of Christ's relationship with the Church.[1] By and through their marriage relationship, they are called to show the church and the world some unique aspect of God's presence and God's love.

Christian married couples have a new vocation within the fundamental Christian vocation they received in baptism. All marriages are holy,[2] but when we talk about Christian marriage we are talking about marriage in Christ. In doing this, we are saying that Christ becomes a third partner in the marriage. His example of love defines Christian marital love as a total giving of self to the other.

Having said this, it should be clear that Christian marriage or the sacrament of matrimony can only be entered into by two baptized persons. The couple marry each other in and though Christ. So our whole theology of marriage does not envision interfaith marriage. In fact, when a Catholic Christian marries an unbaptized person, the permission for the Catholic to do so must first be granted by the local bishop. Further, the pastoral person preparing the couple must attest to the likelihood that the Catholic party will maintain their Christian faith and that the Catholic will do all in her/his power to raise the children of the marriage as Catholics.

While the Church makes a pastoral provision for a marriage of a Catholic to an unbaptized person and sees this marriage as a real marriage and holy, it is clear that this form of marriage is not seen as ideal by the church.

Children of a Jewish-Christian marriage should be taught respect for both traditions. However, if children are to be raised in an historic faith, Judaism or Christianity, that can only be adequately done by raising them in one concrete faith community and with one set of religious symbols and rituals. There is no authentic way one can ask a Jewish-Christian married couple to celebrate together as a family the festivals of Christmas and Easter without watering down or hollowing out the content and mystery of these days. Couples in interfaith marriages, if they really practice their faith, are seriously challenged in having their faith tradition as a binding force in their marriage.

The Church realizes that we do not know how God works in certain human relationships and certain human situations. Because of this the Church makes a pastoral accommodation for those Catholics who experience a vocation, a call from God, to marry an unbaptized person. Certainly, the Jewish partner in such a marriage is welcome to be with his/her children at their sacramental moments; e.g. baptism, first Eucharist, etc. However, as is easily seen, they are always present as observers not participants.

One final point: the Catholic Church is quite sensitive to the impact of the Shoah (Disaster) or Holocaust on the continued existence of the Jewish people. We appreciate that marriage between Jews and non-Jews, in fact, represents yet another threat to ongoing Jewish existence.

1. Ephesians 5:25-33
2. Genesis 2:1

INTERFAITH MARRIAGE
A Jewish View

According to Jewish Law, a marriage cannot be contracted religiously between a Jew and a non-Jew. Therefore, Orthodox,

Conservative and many Reform and Reconstructionist rabbis will not officiate at such wedding ceremonies. This causes a lot of pain in the Jewish community because the percentage of intermarriage is high. Judaism outlawed intermarriage in order to help preserve the integrity of the Jewish faith. In an interfaith marriage, if the children are not brought up Jewish, that line of familial descent going back to Abraham and Sarah is lost. In our day, when our numbers have been so diminished by the Holocaust, this is tragic.

However, even though intermarriage is frowned upon, the children of such a union can be brought up Jewish. Jewish Law recognizes as Jewish, through matrilineal descent, anyone born of a Jewish mother or who ritually converts to Judaism. Reform Judaism broadens this to accept as also Jewish anyone born of a Jewish father, through patrilineal descent, as long as the parents make some positive efforts to raise the child in the Jewish faith. Reconstructionist Judaism also accepts patrilineal descent.

Our hope is that every couple who is considering intermarriage thinks deeply about the consequences of their actions as it affects their future children. Some may decide to bring up their children in the religion of the mother or father. This is good for the children but it leaves one parent as the odd person out, not sharing in the religious identity of the family. If no religion is chosen, the parents deciding to let the children choose for themselves when they grow up, they probably won't choose anything because they have not been fully immersed in either tradition to be able to make a cogent choice. If the parents split the children between both religions, they end up with a split religious identity that is not good for family stability. It fosters closer emotional connection with the parent of the same religion and sometimes causes separation from siblings with a different religious identity. When parents decide to bring up the children in both religions, they face insurmountable barriers. A child cannot be Bar/Bat Mitzvah and receive Holy Communion at the same time. The child has to be either wholly Jewish or wholly Catholic to be brought up in that religion and participate in its sacred rituals.

The best alternative is when one parent converts to the other's religion. That is a deeply personal choice, not one to be taken lightly, because it not only affects the individual, but also, the family from which he/she comes, who may be very hurt by this act of conversion.

This being said, if the parents decide to bring up their children in the Jewish faith then they are welcomed by the Jewish community, even if the non-Jewish parent retains his/her original religious identity. Today Conservative, Reform and Reconstructionist Jews are making special efforts to make intermarried families feel welcome in the synagogue through *Keruv*. This is a Hebrew word that means "bring near." Through Keruv programs, synagogue leaders hope to give young families the feeling that they are definitely wanted by the Jewish community and that their spouse will be socially accepted, even without conversion.

QUESTIONS

Father Cloherty: Since interfaith marriage poses such a threat to Jewish identity and even the future existence of the Jewish people, how do synagogues and Jewish parents promote Jewish marriage while maintaining a stance of openness to Jewish-Christian dialogue?

Rabbi Werb: I don't believe that these two things are mutually exclusive. Although the Jewish community as a whole opposes interfaith marriage, engaging in religious dialogue with people of diverse faiths is not problematic for most Jews. We welcome dialogue because it helps both partners to understand what makes the other unique and what beliefs we share in common. This helps us to strengthen our individual faiths. There is a minority in the Jewish religious community, however, that is skeptical of the efficacy of dialogue. This is based primarily upon the terrible consequences of dialogue in our mutual past history. In medieval times, whenever Jews were called upon by church leaders to engage in any sort of dialogue, it resulted in forced conversion for Jews. You can see why this would leave a bad feeling for some people who are not familiar with the great strides dialogue has taken in modern times. Today, we have real partners in dialogue in the church and we can be comfortable knowing that the end result is not for Jews to give up their faith, but for each side to be illuminated by the other. We have come a long way in Christian-Jewish relations in the past half-century, in large part due to the Second Vatican Council and its landmark proclamation of *Nostra Aetate.*

Rabbi Werb: In an interfaith marriage, does the Catholic partner have to agree to bring up the children in the Catholic faith in order to be married by a Priest?

Father Cloherty: In order to receive the permission (dispensation) from the local bishop to enter a marriage with a non-baptized person, the Catholic party has to promise two things and the non-Catholic party must be made aware of this promise on the part of the Catholic. The Catholic party is to "affirm my faith in Jesus Christ and, with God's help, intend to continue living that faith in the Catholic Church" and to "promise to do *all in my power* to share the faith I have received with our children by having them baptized and reared as Catholics." This promise regarding children highlights again the difficulty of interfaith marriages for an observant Catholic.

CHAPTER 10:

EVIL IN GOD'S WORLD

A Catholic View

On the one hand, a person of faith believes in a good God, who created a universe that is good. On the other hand, that person also experiences both within and outside of himself/herself personal, communal and institutional sinfulness that impacts and influences him/her and others in many ways.

St. Paul, in his letter to the Romans, has a lengthy section on an inner conflict within himself that inclines him and all people to sin.[1] St. Ambrose of Milan tells us that "the law of our fallen nature is at war with the law of reason and subjects the law of reason to the law of error."[2] In these statements, Catholics see the effects of Original Sin on the individual.

A recent form of corporate confession in the Episcopal liturgy includes repentance for "the evil done on our behalf."[3] Such a confession acknowledges a corporate, societal or institutional sinfulness that we may support at least indirectly by our action or lack thereof, e.g. unjust war and great disparities of wealth in our current society.

It is the insight of the 3rd through the 11th chapters of the book of *Genesis* that sinfulness and evil originate in human decisions. Further, it becomes clear that some sinful decisions impact others, subsequent generations and human society. We see this in the sin of Adam and Eve that harms the relationship they have with each other and with God.

This climate of alienation surfaces in Cain's murder of Abel, the decreasing life span of successive generations and the wickedness that leads to the Great Flood and to the Tower of Babel, where pride and an attempt to take God's place divides the human family.

Some sinfulness is personal, and for this we are required to make personal amends to those hurt. However, all sinfulness has community, and perhaps even cosmic, repercussions. Some of these sins can lead to the creation of sinful societal structures.

In 1619, the first slave ship docked at Jamestown in the English colony of Virginia. This event heralded the institution of legalized slavery, which led to a host of evils that still are very present in our society: prejudice, institutional racism, poverty and the deprivation of education for black citizens in the United States.

In a society such as ours, with great economic inequality, there exists among some a mindset that influences policy decisions and attitudes. This mindset promotes the thinking that the poor are poor because they are lazy or even that God intends some to be poor and others to be wealthy. An upper class white person, who is born and raised in a milieu with these kinds of negative attitudes, can uncritically see all of this as normal and just the way it is meant to be.

When the individual is impacted and formed, surrounded as they are by these attitudes and structures, formal or informal, this in itself is not sinful for that individual. There is no personal sin involved at this point. However, once the individual becomes aware through experience, education and ultimately, God's grace that certain attitudes and structures in society are untrue and unjust, then that person is facing a decision.

The decision will be whether or not one will begin to think, speak and act in opposition to these sinful attitudes, structures and institutions or not. Obviously, effective action in this area is usually a result of an organized group effort.

It is widely, if not universally, acknowledged among Christians of our time, that there is a connection between the negative portrayal of Jews in Christian teaching and the Shoah.[4] This connection dates back to the first century. However, while anti-Semitism in Christian teaching was not the complete cause of the Shoah, it certainly added fuel to the fire.

One does not personally make amends for sin that has deep roots in human society in the same way that one does for personal sin. In recent years the Civil Rights Movement, open housing campaigns, grass-roots community organizing etc. have given many of us concrete ways to begin to make amends for the past and current sinful treatment of Blacks and the poor by our society. When we join with others to create a more just society and challenge the lies that cause people to live lives approaching human desperation, these efforts counter what we, as Catholics, see as the impact of Original Sin and attempt to move this world in the direction of the Reign of God. Albert Camus, the French existential philosopher and novelist (1913-1960), described the outlines of these efforts well. He once described the moral challenge of his generation as, "If not to reduce evil, at least not to add to it." "Perhaps we cannot prevent this world from being a world in which children are tortured. But we can reduce the number of tortured children."[5]

Beyond all this, Catholic Christians hold that while human nature in itself is good, there is in us all a fundamental inclination to sin that is passed on to us just by our being born as humans. In chapter 5, in my answer to Rabbi Werb's question, "What is Original Sin and how do Catholics make amends for it?" I made reference to St. Paul's comment in his *Letter to the Romans* 7:14-24, as well as the teaching of the Council of Trent, which taught that Original Sin is passed down "by propagation and not just imitation." The last two paragraphs of this answer to Rabbi Werb at the end of chapter 5 are relevant here.

Much of the above is concerned with moral evil and the strands of evil that exist in institutions because of human action or inaction. However, there are other evils, some of which are sickness, natural disasters and accidents that cause great harm. I believe that Rabbi Werb has some good reflections on this in his part of this chapter. Also, Rabbi Harold Kushner's book, *When Bad Things Happen to Good People*, dwells on this subject in a thought-provoking manner.

1. Romans 7:14-25

2. The Liturgy of the Hours Vol. IV Pg. 1538

3. Weavings Vol. XXVII, #1, Pg. 44

4. Shoah, Hebrew for disaster, the preferred term for the Holocaust.

5. Robert Ellsberg, *All Saints* Pg. 48

EVIL IN GOD'S WORLD
A Jewish View

The subject of Theodicy, evil in God's good world, is a vexing one. If God is good, as we believe, why does He cause evil or, at the very least, why does He allow it to exist? This is a conundrum that goes back to Biblical times and is the subject matter of the book of *Job*. The author of Job wrestles with this question and answers it by pointing out that God is omnipotent. He creates all things, both those that are good and those that we conceive as evil. In *Isaiah* too we are told, "I form light and create darkness, I make peace and create evil."[1] God is, thus, the source of all creation and we human beings cannot totally understand the purpose of evil.

Many people believe that Satan, synonymous with the Devil, is the source of all evil. Satan is introduced in Job as a scheming, cunning character. He has no real personal identity, however, and is referred to in Hebrew as "hasatan," the tempter. He merely serves as God's literary foil, in the prologue of the book, carrying out His plan to cause Job misery and suffering. God's power, however, is supreme. Job's friends offer the universally accepted answer at that time to human suffering, i.e. that it is punishment for sin against God. Job, in proclaiming his rightful innocence, maintains that his suffering is not due to anything that he did wrong. He is blameless. In this way Job represents countless numbers of people, even today, who feel that the terrible tragedies thrust upon them have no redeeming merit, questioning God's goodness as a result. Some may agree with the answer offered by the book of Job that in the end we are truly ignorant of the totality of God's work in the world and we must just accept God's inscrutable will, without questioning why. Yet Abraham, in the book of *Genesis*, confronts God when he hears that He is going to destroy the cities of Sodom and Gomorra with the challenging words, "Shall not the Judge of all the earth do justly?"[2] Abraham expects God to act justly because the hallmark of His presence in the world is justice. God too must be subject to his own moral code. But this doesn't always seem to be the case.

We are nurtured since childhood by our individual faiths to thank God for all of the good in our lives. When we are confronted by tragic circumstances, however, we hit a brick wall theologically. We don't know where to turn. Some say it is God's will and we cannot question His wisdom. Others blame God for the evil that confronts them and turn away from God.

I would prefer to understand evil in God's world in a different manner. God created us with freewill, which is the underlying meaning of the Garden of Eden story. When man disobeys God and does evil, he suffers the consequences. Unfortunately, these consequences sometimes have a spill over effect upon people who are not, themselves, guilty. Evil tends to overrun all in its path. If he obeys God then goodness ensues and all people benefit. Man has the freedom to choose. He is not a puppet forced to do God's will. God created a good world. That was his master plan at the beginning of Genesis. Man, however, disobeyed God and brought evil into the world in the form of the first murder. When man killed his brother, God did not stop it, as He does not stop any tragedy, because He would then upset the order of nature that He created. He allows evil to exist because He gave humans the freedom to choose good or evil.[3] Thus, we cannot say that God caused the Shoah, the Holocaust, one of the most heinous evils in the history of the world. Rather, it was human, deliberate action that brought it about. It was the result of human freewill. The atrocities and barbaric acts that resulted in the brutal deaths of 6 million Jews were perpetrated by human beings, the Nazis and their collaborators. Their horrible deeds were acceptable to many because of a deep seated hatred and prejudice that was percolating in the collective European consciousness for centuries. In fact, most of the history of Medieval times reflects man's inhumanity to man. Anti-semitism was the norm of the day. Sadly, church teachings of supersessionism aided and abetted the Jew hatred that was common in those days, as Father Cloherty has underscored. Also, the erroneous belief that Jews were "Christ killers" resulted in the horrible deaths of untold numbers of innocent Jews. The modern evolution of many of those destructive beliefs and terrible human actions was the Shoah.

Black slavery is another terrible evil that was not caused by God. Human slave traders, white and black, spread slavery throughout the world and human slave owners helped to perpetuate this vile condition that kept Black people suffering horribly for generations. Prejudice against African-Americans, tragically, continues to exist today and the effects of slavery are still being felt in our society.

The horrible Armenian genocide, the ravages of

Communism, the brutality of modern terrorism and the tragic loss of life in various wars are, also, products of human hatred and evil, not actions of God.

Of course, there is other evil in our world not caused by human beings. Natural catastrophes, such as hurricanes, typhoons, floods, earthquakes, volcanoes and tsunamis cause untold damage and suffering. Once again, God does not stop these occurrences because they are part of the natural order of the universe. Rather, it is our responsibility to stay out of the path of natural upheavals. This is not always possible, but when tragedy occurs we cannot blame it on God, but upon the impersonal forces of nature.

On the evening of September 4, 1972, eight members of the Palestinian terror group Black September murdered eleven Israeli Olympic athletes in Munich, Germany. This vile event became known as "the Munich massacre." In commenting on this tragedy one of my Hebrew High School students, Craig Mendelson, wrote perceptively a few weeks later:

"On this day of Yom Kippur I am surrounded by the crying and tears of my fellowmen. I hear mankind scream out their indignation at the injustices inflicted upon them. I hear them cry out, why God, why? But wait! Isn't there something wrong? Shouldn't the tearful question be, why mankind, why?

"Did God pull the trigger eleven times? The important question is where is man's responsibility in these injustices?

Where does man's responsibility stop when the tragedy of Munich ceases to be front page news? Did God really inflict these injustices upon us, or rather, did we inflict them upon Him?"

This latter question that Craig poses is very perceptive for a young man. Unfortunately, and very sadly, Craig's own promising life was cut short a year later by a terrible illness, which in itself, leaves us with many further theological questions.

Disease and accidents test our belief in God's goodness. God does not cause these terrible happenings, either. They occur naturally and haphazardly. As human beings we must support medical research and work diligently to find the cure for diseases that wrack our bodies and cause pain and death. We need to be more careful in driving cars and other modes of transportation so as not to place ourselves in dangerous situations. Even when it is not our fault, it is human error that causes accidents, not God.

We might ask why did God create such a world where terrible things can occur? Why is death the ultimate end? To this we have no cogent answer because we cannot read the mind of God. However, our Jewish tradition teaches that when the children of the righteous die in the lifetime of their parents, even God is grieved.[4] God feels our pain and shares our suffering. Rabbi Harold Kushner points out that God is with us when we "walk through the valley of the shadow of death." That gives us some measure of comfort. The other belief that helps sustain us is that in the afterlife God rectifies the wrongs of this world, rewarding the innocent and punishing the wicked, thus balancing the scales of cosmic justice. The afterlife is God's reward for the trials and tribulations of this world.

This belief is an important one when we think about the abject evil of the Holocaust, which truly tests our faith in God. Neither that God cannot intervene to stop evil nor that He consciously chooses not to stop evil are totally satisfactory theories because the first limits God's power and the second implies that He is evil, too. A God who is not all-powerful is not much of a God and one who chooses not to stop evil is worthless. Even if God is self-limiting in order to grant us freewill, as I believe, we are still troubled when confronted with very difficult and challenging circumstances in our lives, by God's seeming absence.

Although we may not have an all-encompassing answer to the problem of evil in God's world, if we believe in a God of goodness then the afterlife helps us to better accept the harsh reality of life on this physical plane of existence. In the end, however, after all of our speculations on this difficult subject, we must refer back to the book of Job and accept the realization that there are some things that are beyond human understanding and the problem of evil is one of them.

1. Isaiah 45:7

2. Genesis 18:23-25

3. Deuteronomy 30:15

4. Midrash Rabbah 2:24

QUESTIONS

Father Cloherty: It would seem to me from your statement that we have a common approach in faith to the existence of evil in a world created by a good God. While justice is essential for Christians, the element of mercy extends even to the most outrageous sinners. What are your thoughts on that?

Rabbi Werb: It is very difficult for us to conceive of mercy for tyrants, mass murderers, Nazis, rapists, terrorists and those who have perpetrated unspeakable crimes against others, such as beheadings and burning people alive. As much as God is merciful, He is also just. Heinous crimes cry out for justice for the persecuted, even more than mercy for the oppressors, especially, when they do not even ask for forgiveness themselves. Our secular legal system is predicated on the premise of "justice for all." The world that we live in, however, is one in which evil often goes unpunished. This is why we trust in God's goodness, mercy and justice to balance the scales in His own way in the afterlife.

Rabbi Werb: Do Catholics believe in freewill or are all our actions, good and evil, preordained by God?

Father Cloherty: The second and third chapters of the book of *Genesis* present human persons as free. In Genesis 2:16 and 17, God gives them a command: they are not to eat from the tree of the knowledge of good and evil. Then in Genesis 3:6, our first parents disobey that command. The fact that they are punished for this disobedience indicates that they freely chose to disobey. If this were not so, their punishment would be unjust.

It is our daily experience that we are free. However, the disciplines of sociology and psychology have taught us that sometimes we are not as free as we might think. We are conditioned by our family background and inherited DNA, as well as the culture and pre-suppositions of our environment and society.

Furthermore, there are places in Scripture that seem to indicate that God has determined all things from eternity. The Prophet Isaiah, speaking for God, writes: "At the beginning I foretell the outcome in advance, things not done. I say that my plan shall stand; I accomplish every purpose."[1]

Medieval philosophers debated this seeming tension between human freewill and God's knowledge of the future. I see no possible resolution to this debate. I would hold both to human freedom, which at times can be limited, as suggested above, and God's knowledge of the future. These two cannot be logically reconciled. I suppose I have reached the age where it doesn't bother me that some things are beyond human logic.

1. Isaiah 46:1

Further Questions
for Our Readers:

Revelation (Chap. 1)

Since Jews and Christians agree that God is immanent, fully present to us, as well as transcendent, beyond us, how would you say God has revealed Himself to you? Is there a personal story that illustrates your experience?

God, One and Three? (Chap. 2)

The admonition in *Exodus* 20:1-6 (Ten Commandments) and for Jews, the daily recitation of the Shema Yisrael (Hear, O Israel, the Lord our God, the Lord is one), are clear admonitions against idolatry and false gods. How do you see idolatry operating in our society today?

Messiah (Chap. 3)

Since the coming of the Messiah is part of the core teaching of our two faith traditions, what practices and teachings can we learn from each other to help prepare the way for the Messiah?

Religious Authority (Chap. 4)

Given the differences in teaching authority between Judaism and Catholic Christianity, do you see any common process in making decisions about faith and practice? How does conscience play a role in decision making?

Sin (Chap. 5)

How do we effect reconciliation with our fellow human being when we have sinned against him/her?

Salvation (Chap. 6)

Can a person who doesn't believe in God experience salvation?

Life after Death (Chap. 7)

Do you believe that Catholics and Jews will share eternity together, even though our theological beliefs differ?

Angels (Chap. 8)

Have you ever had any personal experience of an angel communicating with you? What kind of experience might people have today that could be attributed to an angel?

Interfaith Marriage (Chap. 9)

Do you believe that interfaith marriage is a threat to either Catholic or Jewish identity? How do we address this issue in today's world?

Evil in God's World (Chap. 10)

As Catholics and Jews we have a responsibility from our faith traditions to eradicate evil. How do we begin to do this?

Afterword:
Interfaith Dialogue

by

Father Cloherty

I grew up in the late 1930s and the 1940s in the Jamaica Plain part of Boston. Most of the adults in my neighborhood were Irish Catholic immigrants. However, at the end of my street there lived a very large community of people who were clearly different from us. They were Jews. The fact that they were really somehow different intrigued me. I never reflected upon it growing up because children from that community and our Irish Catholic community never played together. It surely was not a matter of class differences based on income or wealth. The adults in both communities had similar types of employment. Many, like my parents, were immigrants.

In those days, in my home at some point on Sunday evenings, "our" radio programs – The Shadow, George Burns and Gracie Allen and Inner Sanctum – were turned off and we "had" to listen to the "Irish Hour." That hour was preceded by "The

Joseph Tall Hour," a program of Jewish music. At times, when I heard the end of that program and listened to that music, I thought to myself that it was the music of the people at the top of the hill.

After ordination in 1962, I met a few rabbis and worked well with them on community issues. I also participated in Interfaith Thanksgiving Services. But any attempts at dialogue on faith issues never seemed to go anywhere. I could never understand that.

In 1992, I was assigned to St. Patrick's Parish in Brockton, Massachusetts. I served at that parish and then at Lady of Lourdes Parish in Brockton until 2011. In 1993, I was invited to join the Catholic-Jewish Dialogue Committee at Stonehill College in North Easton. There I met H. David Werb, then the Rabbi at Temple Beth Emunah in Brockton. At those early meetings I noticed that, as vital as it was and still is, study of the effects of anti-Semitism seemed to be the sole agenda item of the committee. Surely, that topic was of interest and value, but frankly, I was more interested in why anti-Semitism exists? Were there ways that Christians thought and taught about Jews that led to anti-Semitism and, perhaps, even the Shoah? I began to push for dialogue on matters of faith, but the committee resisted. At one meeting, as I once again pushed for faith based dialogue, Rabbi Werb asked a question for which I was not prepared: "Has the Catholic Church changed its position on the Jews?"

Over the years, I had collected numerous volumes on Christian-Jewish relations, but having no rabbi with whom to dialogue they went unread. In the summer of 1993, I plunged into that unread material. As a result, when the Catholic-Jewish Committee met again in the fall I was ready for Rabbi Werb's question, "Has the Catholic Church changed its position on the Jews?" When he once again posed that question, I told him that I too had a question for him. First, however, I told him that the reason I wanted to get into a dialogue on faith with him was that I hoped, thereby, to better appreciate and understand the God that the Jew, Jesus of Nazareth, worshipped. If I understood his (Rabbi Werb's) thinking and faith about God, this would help me. So, "Yes," I answered, "it does seem to me that we Catholics have changed and are still changing our position on the Jews, but here is my question: 'Do you, Rabbi Werb, think that you have anything to learn about God from me?'" He then said: "Let me say two things and then answer your question. First, we Jews and Christians have a terrible history together and there is a real question of trust. Second, when Christians have engaged us in religious dialogue in the past the purpose was either to humiliate or convert us. However, it seems clear to me that you are truly interested in interfaith dialogue and you are not trying to convert me. So, in answer to your question, yes, I do believe that I have something to learn about God from you." These words began our many years of dialogue together.

My discussions at the Catholic-Jewish Committee at Stonehill College and with Rabbi Werb have been a major step in my long search to better understand and appreciate the people whom I first encountered in Jamaica Plain as a child and whose music I first heard on "The Joseph Tall Hour." I would say that this book is for me one very concrete and wonderful fruit of that search to understand and connect with a people that I now understand is different, but with whom I share so much. I am particularly grateful to the Catholic-Jewish Committee members and, especially, to David Werb, for their trust and openness without which this book would not be possible.

Afterword:
Interfaith Dialogue

by

Rabbi Werb

Interfaith dialogue between Christians and Jews has been going on for a long time. Today, we take it pretty much for granted. For the most part, however, this dialogue has centered on issues of social conscience. I, myself, was involved in such dialogues through various clergy groups that I belonged to during my active rabbinical career. In Brockton, Massachusetts, where I served for 36 years in the pulpit at Temple Beth Emunah, I had the privilege of being a part of the Brockton Interfaith Community (BIC), a social action dialogue group composed of a cross section of various religious, ethnic and racial groups within the community. This organization is still doing very important work revolving around jobs, housing, after school programs, safety, poverty, raising the minimum wage, etc. Through BIC, I came to have a better understanding of my fellow citizens on the human level and made many good friends. It is because of my involvement with BIC that our congregation still sponsors an annual program for the community on the birthday weekend of Dr. Martin Luther King, Jr. I also had the opportunity to host many visits by local pastors who brought church youth classes and adult congregants to our synagogue to learn about the roots of Christianity in Judaism. I became so friendly with the local pastors that one time, when one of my neighboring colleagues was recuperating from knee surgery, he asked me, of all people, to lead services in his church on Sunday morning in his absence. That was quite something for a rabbi to conduct services in a Protestant Church, an experience I will never forget.

It wasn't, however, until the early '90's when the Catholic Jewish Dialogue committee was formed by Professor James Kenneally at Stonehill College in neighboring North Easton that I really started to engage in theological dialogue. It was there that I met Father Frank Cloherty, who, at that time, was Pastor at St. Patrick's Parish in Brockton. We discussed many topics at the monthly sessions that related to matters of faith and belief. This was the first time that I had the opportunity to explore theological issues with people of Catholic faith. At first I was hesitant to speak candidly because I didn't know what the reaction would be on the part of the Catholic participants, but soon Father Cloherty and I began to feel comfortable talking about any topic that was on the table. We often got into some lengthy discussions, which probably tried the patience of some of the other participants.

Out of our contact at Stonehill College grew our mutual desire to expand our dialogue and involve our own congregants and parishioners. So we brought together groups from the church and synagogue to get acquainted with each other and to learn from each other. We taught classes at both the church and the synagogue, bringing together our people for dialogue. On numerous occasions I had the honor of preaching at Mass and Father Cloherty, in turn, delivered homilies at our Sabbath services.

I must admit that when I first went into a church it was an emotional experience. I wondered to myself whether I was betraying my fellow Jews, who for almost 2,000 years had been rejected, vilified and persecuted by Christians because they didn't believe in Jesus. Were these Catholic Christians still clinging to the belief that the ultimate goal of dialogue was our conversion? Father Cloherty, however, made it quite clear that there were no strings attached to our relationship. Vatican II, through its revolutionary statement about the Jews in *Nostra Aetate*, paved the way for Catholics and Jews to explore each others' faith in a sincere, forthright manner. *Nostra Aetate* makes it quite clear that Jesus' patrimony stems from Judaism and that the Virgin Mary, as well as the Apostles and most of Jesus' disciples, were all Jews. It explicitly "decries hatred, persecutions, displays of anti-Semitism directed against Jews at any time and by anyone." The Jews are described as "most dear" to God and the document denies that Jews could be held collectively responsible for Jesus' death. "What happened in His passion cannot be charged against all the Jews, without distinction, then alive, nor against the Jews of today. The Jews should not be presented as rejected or accursed by God, as if this followed from the Holy Scriptures." That the Jews were responsible for the crucifixion of Jesus has fueled the fires of anti-semitism for the past two thousand years as underscored by such noted authors as Edward Flannery,[1] James Carroll,[2] William Nichols,[3] and Solomon Zeitlin.[4] By exonerating the Jewish people from this disastrous charge, the Catholic Church has opened the door to dialogue. Furthermore, in the working document of 1969 put out by the Holy See's office for Catholic-Jewish relations entitled *Reflections and Suggestions for the Application of the Directives of Nostra Aetate*, it states quite clearly that in regard to the Jews, "all intent of proselytizing and conversion is excluded."

Pope Francis has expressed the Church's current teaching on Judaism in his apostolic exhortation of Nov. 24, 2013, Evangel Gaudium (The Joy of the Gospel), as follows:

"247. We hold the Jewish people in special regard because their covenant with God has never been revoked, for 'the gifts and the call of God are irrevocable' (*Rom* 11:29). The Church, which shares with Jews an important part of the sacred Scriptures, looks upon the people of the covenant and their faith as one of the sacred roots of her own Christian identity (cf. *Rom* 11:16-18). As Christians, we cannot consider Judaism as a foreign religion; nor do we include the Jews among those called to turn from idols and to serve the true God (cf. *1 Thes* 1:9). With them, we believe in the one God who acts in history, and with them we accept his revealed word. 248. Dialogue and friendship with the children of Israel are part of the life of Jesus' disciples. The friendship which has grown between us makes us bitterly and sincerely regret the terrible persecutions which they have endured, and continue to endure, especially those that have involved Christians. 249. God continues to work among the people of the Old Covenant and to bring forth treasures of wisdom which flow from their encounter with his word. For this reason, the Church also is enriched when she receives the values of Judaism. While it is true that certain Christian beliefs are unacceptable to Judaism, and that the Church cannot refrain from proclaiming Jesus as Lord and Messiah, there exists as well a rich complementarity which allows us to read the texts of the Hebrew Scriptures together and to help one another to mine the riches of God's word. We can also share many ethical convictions and a common concern for justice and the development of peoples."

Recently, I had the wonderful opportunity to hear Professor John Connelly of the University of California at Berkeley lecture at Stonehill College on his book, *From Enemy to Brother: The Revolution in Catholic Teaching on the Jews,*

1933-1965. This book documents the evolution in Catholic thinking from the 1930's with the rise of Hitler to 1965 when the revolutionary statement on the Jews in *Nostra Aetate* was first promulgated by the Catholic Church at the Vatican II Church Council. Although, the prime mover for this alteration of Catholic views on the Jews was Pope John XXIII, a number of other theologians were instrumental over a period of three decades in changing the 17 centuries old perception of the Jews from enemies of the church to "older brothers" in faith. The earlier view of the Jews as enemies led to tremendous persecution of Jews in the society at large. The new perception of the Jews has led to dialogue and understanding. This is underscored in *Nostra Aetate* in the following words: "Since the spiritual patrimony common to Christians and Jews is thus so great, this sacred synod wants to foster and recommend that mutual understanding and respect which is the fruit, above all, of biblical and theological studies as well as of fraternal dialogues."

These dialogues have been taking place on the international, national and local levels between organizational representatives, as well as among plain ordinary people. As a result of *Nostra Aetate*, Jews have been able to engage in dialogue, not only with Catholics but with Protestants, too. Now, the door has also been opened to begin dialogue in some communities with Muslim leaders. This bodes well for the possibility of mutual understanding between people of various faiths and may ultimately help to bring about peace and goodwill among former adversaries. This is our hope and prayer for the ultimate results of dialogue.

I believe that my relationship with Father Cloherty is a sterling example of the fruits of dialogue, and I am indebted to him for our loving collaboration and many months of work together on this book.

1. The Anguish Of the Jews: Twenty Three Centuries of Antisemitism, 2004, Paulist Press (paperback, first published 1965).

2. Constantine's Sword: The Church and the Jews, A History, 2001, Houghton Miflin Harcourt.

3. Christian Antisemitism: A History of Hate, 1993, Jason Aronson, Inc.

4. Who Crucified Jesus, 1964, Bloch Publishing Company.

57578561R00086

Made in the USA
Middletown, DE
01 August 2019